THE SECRET OF GOOD HEALTH - OLIVE OIL

Translation: **Maria Bitsakaki-Psilaki**
           Melanie Godwin

Photographs: Nikos Psilakis
(The photographs on p. 9, 10 (above) and 71 have kindly been donated by Michalis Nikiphorakis. The pictures of the fossilized olive leaves (p.10) have been provided by Prof. Evang. Velitzelos.

Layout: Nikos Dretakis

Printing: TYPOKRETA
Bookbinding: Z. Mouthatsakis, Skoteino, Pethiatha

ISBN: 960-7448-18-9

NIKOS & MARIA
PSILAKIS

The secret of good health
Olive Oil

Advice on its correct use

KARMANOR
Under the Auspices
of the Greek Academy of Taste

CONTENTS

THE OLIVE TREE AND ITS OIL
IN PREHISTORIC TIMES

For thousands of years now, the inhabitants of the Mediterranean countries have cultivated the olive tree and used its products for their daily needs. The edible olives and oil were used in their food, the leaves and the oil had therapeutic powers or were used as incense and the oil was also used as an offering to the gods.

Greeks based their diet on olive products for thousands of years. On Crete, in the south of the Peloponnese, on the islands of the Aegean and in many other areas, olive oil was almost exclusively used as the fat content in food. This is why the olive tree is such a beloved tree, blessed by God himself and seen as holy, in the eyes of Greek folklore tradition.

The olive tree has its origins in the Mediterranean and greatly influenced the formation of a civilization in a place where some of the earliest human civilizations were developed. Charming old and newer legends, along with ancient customs which still survive, prove without doubt the connection of the olive tree with both ancient and later forms of worship. The development of a civilization can be seen through the people's diet. The identity of an area is shaped by the goods that are produced there. Wheat, wine and olive oil are the main products of Greece. All three are blessed and they have been used as a part of holy worship for thousands of years.

An olive grove on Crete.

The cultivation of grain crops shows the evolution of society, a system whereby a farmer stored food that was collected, in order to attain an established standard of living. The pressing of olives and the extraction of olive oil came much later, when mankind had developed a higher form of civilization which was characterized by the development of technology... The machinery that was invented for use in the processing of food products are maybe the first ones invented by the human mind.

The trunk of a centuries-old olive tree.

THE OLIVE TREE - 60,000 YEARS OLD

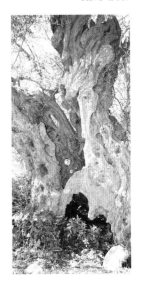

❋ But when did the olive tree appear? The tree, indigenous to the Mediterranean area, seems to have been around for thousands of years. A fossilized leaf of the *olea noti* family has been found at Kyme on Euboea, while evidence which proves the scattered spreading out of the tree has been found in Provence in France and in the countries of Northern Africa. This extremely old piece of evidence fills you with awe for the antiquity of this tree. It originates from the islands of the Aegean, Santorini and Nisyros, where professor Evangelos Velitzelos discovered

A Greek hill planted all over with olive trees.

Fossilized olive leaves. They have been found by prof. Evangelos Velitzelos on the Aegean islands.

fossilized olive tree leaves aged fifty to sixty thousands years old! Experts on Palaeobotany believe that what was discovered were leaves of cultivated olive trees.

Different researchers have so far offered a range of opinions on the cultivation and the spread of the olive tree in the Mediterranean and the Middle East region. The ancestor of the cultivated olive tree is usually believed to be a variety of the still well-known wild olive tree which can readily be seen on Crete, in the Peloponnese and in other areas of Southern Greece, Northern Africa and the Middle East. All this supports the theory that the modern Mediterranean olive tree comes from the plant *olea chrysophylla*.

At some point in prehistoric times, mankind in the Mediterranean did not like the potluck method of gathering olives, which were used in his diet and might even have produced oil, so he looked for a systematic way of cultivating olive trees. In other words, man organized the production of olives and so most probably olive oil, either by cultivating olive trees or by domesticating the, then wild, indigenous olive tree. This was a long and laborious process. It

An olive grove on Crete in the Minoan period. Fresco from the palace of Cnossos depicting "the sacred grove" (17th-16th c. B.C.).

is felt that Crete is the area which started the systematic cultivation of the olive tree. The French researcher Paul Faure strongly believes that the inhabitants of Neolithic Crete were the ones who started the cultivation of olive trees: *"The honour of having domesticated wild olive trees into ones that were cultivated, belongs to the villagers of the great island of Crete"*, he emphasized.

MINOAN CRETE

Evidence from Crete in the third millennium before Christ is quite clear as far as the use of edible olives and olive oil is concerned. The archaeological excavations led by P. Warren at Myrtos in Ierapetra uncovered important information about the systematic cultivation of olive trees in the area in the Early Bronze Age (Early Minoan Period, 2800-2100 B.C.). The single olive stone which was found in the digs is believed to have come from a domesticated olive tree, while most of the wood found in the area was olive tree wood. During that period, people still used olive tree wood for building and maybe for the

Jars for the storage of olive oil and other products from the palaces of Cnossos and Phaestos.

making of furniture in their houses. Olives from the same period have also been found at Cnossos.

Evidence from subsequent years is even more enlightening. In the Middle Bronze Age (Middle Minoan Period, 2100-1560 B.C.), the cultivation of olive trees was one of the basic occupations of the inhabitants. In the archaeological excavations which were headed by J. and E. Sakellarakis at Fourni in Archanes, a bowl containing charred olive stones was discovered next to an earthenware jar which could have been possibly used for the storage of agricultural products. In two other pots there were the charred remains of figs and vetch, whilst scattered around, close at hand, were burnt chickpeas and broad beans. Oil lamps which were found during the Cretan archaeological digs, prove the earliest use of olive oil for lighting. Olives and olive oil seem to have been of great economic importance in the Minoan

Representation of an olive tree on a fresco at Cnossos.

world. The French researcher Paul Faure believed this point to such an extent that he stated that *"the olive tree ensured the economic dominance of Crete in the Aegean World"*.

EDIBLE OLIVES – 3500 YEARS OLD!

An impressive archaeological discovery bears witness to the relationship between the edible olive in cooking and in worship. Archaeologists who carried out excavations on Crete, in the area of Zakros on the east side of the island, have uncovered olives aged 3500 years! These olives looked fresh since they had retained their skins. The city had been destroyed due to an earthquake before 3500 years. Archaeologists have given a logical reason for this finding. A short while before the disastrous earthquake which finally brought down the palace, during the pre-earthquake tremors that had already started (a warning of the forthcoming disaster), offerings were made to the gods in the form of bowls filled with edible olives. It was judged that the most suitable place for this offering was a well. The people probably believed that by placing the offerings in the well, they would be closer to the powers of the underworld, the same ones that could cause such strong earth tremors. When archaeologists uncovered the well, a bowl full of olives was found and they too, had kept their skins after so many years! A few minutes after their discovery the olives disintegrated but thankfully, the archaeologists managed to take pictures of them. *"I was down in the well and we were looking around the water. Suddenly my hand fell on a bowl which contained both dry and slimy things. We took the bowl out and to our joy, saw that there were olives in it, not very big but shiny ones"*.

The olives which were found in an ancient well at Zakros, Crete, after 3,500 years!

Ancient people used to place their offerings to the gods of the underworld in holes or hollows in the earth.

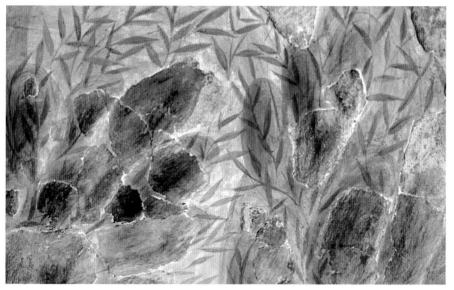

Fresco from Cnossos depicting an olive tree. Below:Gold amulets in the shape of olive tree leaves from Mochlos.

OLIVES IN GRAVES!

※ The importance of the olive tree and olive oil before 1500 B.C. can be seen in the burial customs of that period. Archaeologists have found stones of edible olives next to human remains in graves. Perhaps people at that time believed that this valuable food was needed by the dead in the next world. They may even have thought that it was necessary for the long journey the dead would take.

OLIVE TREES IN MINOAN ART

※ The olive and its role in the economy, diet and worship is further typified by the eloquence of Minoan and Mycenaean art. It seems that by the third millennium before Christ, people had already made golden amulets in the shape of olive tree leaves, which were found in graves at Mochlos in Sitia. Equally impressive is the olive branch which can be seen in the hair of the girl gathering crocuses which is depicted in a

An olive sprig in the hair of a young woman from Akrotiri, Santorini.

fresco that was found at Akrotiri in Thera. It could be said that the olive tree dominated in the Minoan world which was full of light and colour and gave valuable pictures of daily life!

OLIVES
AND OLIVE OIL
IN IDEOGRAMS

Ideograms symbolizing olive oil, the olive tree and olive fruit in Linear B script, around 1400 B.C

Tablet with ideograms referring to offers of olive oil to the gods.

※ Around 2000 B.C. people used symbols (ideograms) for olive trees and olive oil. This ancient type of writing is known as Linear A. In the still unpublished work by Menas Tzikritzis, it is claimed that on offering tables from southern Crete dated back to the 18th century B.C., ideograms of olive trees and olive oil can be read next to the name Athena, the Greek goddess who is believed to have first planted the olive tree. The same ideogram or symbol can still be seen after the destruction of the Minoan civilization. Linear A tablets which were found in Archanes show ideograms which describe different types of food. Among those are ideograms depicting olive trees, olive oil, wheat and wine.

People in ancient times continued to write on clay tablets after the fall of the Minoan civilization. The tablets written after 1450 B.C. were different from their predecessors. Following the Second World War, an ingenious English cryptologist, Michael Ventris, managed to decipher them. In this way, he offered a valuable gift to the world, as it shed light on life two thousand years before Christ. There are

Tablet with ideograms. It refers to olive groves.

many points of evidence which indicate both olive trees and olive oil. People of that time not only cultivated olive trees but also scented their oil with herbs. They produced aromatic oil and this was offered along with the non-scented oil to the gods. On one of the tablets there is even an olive shown as a form of food.

The ideograms with which the Minoans and later the Mycenaeans declared their olive oil in a shorthand type are quite impressive. People at Cnossos used a symbol very similar to the olive tree itself. The ideogram which represents the olive looks like an olive tree flower and a special ideogram was used for the olive oil.

Tripod Minoan pot. Recent analyses proved that ancient people cooked food in them using olive oil even before 2000 B.C.

OLIVE OIL IN MINOAN COOKING POTS!

❋ The Minoans and the people of the Mycenaean period, during the second and third millennium before Christ, used olive oil for practical as well as religious purposes. As far as the cooking uses are concerned, we now have quite a good idea, even though there is no written evidence. A chemical analysis of a Minoan utensil which was carried out recently, showed that the people of that time used olive oil in their cooking! Tablets found at Cnossos record deliveries of oil along with other basic food products, such as barley, figs, wine, honey and possibly flour, which were sent out to unknown receivers, maybe even members of some kind of priesthood.

Linear B tablet. It refers to olive oil scented with coriander.

SCENTED OIL IN PREHISTORY
NAMES OF OIL SCENTERS

Scented oil is referred to on several occasions in the Linear B tablets. Names of people who scented the oil are even mentioned. Eumedes, Thyestas, Cocalus and Philaeus were oil scenters from Pylos in the Peloponnese. It is well known that they used aromatic plants in the preparation of scents ("orthoen", "sfakoen", "kyperoen" were oils scented with rose petals, sage and cyperus accordingly). In Pylos, the oil was categorized into six or more groups depending on its scent, date or area of production and what use it would be put to. Clay tablets at Cnossos refer to oil from Lyctos being scented with coriander. Lyctos was a wonderful city in central Crete. All these factors point to an advanced knowledge in oil industry. The ancient people of Crete knew how to separate olives of varying type and quality or how to extract the ethereal oils and scent the olive oil with them.

HOMERIC TIMES

The olive tree seems to have had its own special role in daily life in Homeric times. Homer, the famous poet of ancient Greece, left us with two enormously important poems with regards to human civilization, in which there is interesting information about the olive tree and its oil. It is said in the poems that in the gardens of Alkinoos, the king of the Phaeakae, there were olive trees along with other trees which had edible fruits. It is also stated that olive wood was used in the making of furniture. Odysseus, the hero who roamed the seas for ten years, built his bed from olive wood. Edible olives and scented oil were well known in Homeric times. The spe-  cially prepared oil was used in caring for the body as well as the bodies of the dead. Even Aphrodite, the beautiful goddess of love, used rose-scented oil when she annointed Hector's dead body, one of the leading characters in the Trojan war.

Olive harvesting in ancient times.

The goddess Athena plants the first olive tree on the Acropolis, as described in the beautiful ancient myth.

THE OLIVE TREE AND ITS OIL
IN THE CLASSICAL PERIOD

Information about the olive tree and its oil has become more readily available as the years went by. As society developed, the olive tree became more valuable. Moreover, measures were taken to protect these trees. It is known that the olive tree was cultivated and protected by particular laws in Athens. In 5th century B.C., the Athenians introduced special measures to protect olive trees while at the same time, there were sacred trees which were believed to have descended from the very same olive trees that Athena, the goddess of wisdom, had planted on the holy rock of the Acropolis. This was believed to have been the first olive tree to have been planted in the world! Zeus, the great god of the Greeks, was the protector of these holy trees. These trees were, at the beginning, planted at Academia, in the "sacred grove", but later they were cultivated in various other areas in Attica.

"Everyone has to plant an olive tree..."

In an ancient Cretan town known as Dreros, which was to be found close by to today's Aghios Nikolaos, an ancient inscription has been discovered which includes a grave oath. This oath obliges every young man to plant at least one olive tree and to look after it until it has fully grown. This custom seems to have been the practice in other towns, too. It is highly possible that this was the main ritual in an initiation into a social group.

THE ROMAN AND BYZANTINE PERIODS

During Roman times, olive oil became much more widely known in many areas. The enormous Roman Empire often undertook measures to ensure that its citizens did not suffer from a shortage of olive oil. Not only the import to Rome but also its distribution was overseen. Trade developed rapidly and Roman ships transported large quantities of olive oil to areas where the olive tree was not cultivated or to places where a small production of oil did not meet the demands of the locals.

The cultivation of olive trees continued for many centuries to be one of the main forms of occupation for the inhabitants of Greece. With regards to the Byzantine period, we have many useful pieces of information, both direct and indirect, which have helped us to find out more about large-scale production of olive oil in certain areas, such as the Peloponnese. After the fall of the Byzantine Empire in 1453 A.D., the olive became the symbol of survival for the inhabitants of many agricultural areas. Living under extremely difficult conditions, these people found a relatively easy product which could be put to many uses and so ensured their survival. Information which has been

Olive harvesting in Byzantium. Detail from an illustrated Byzantine manuscript.

Olive harvesting on the island of Lesbos. A picture by the popular painter Theophilus.

saved bears witness to the fact that people used olive oil in cooking on a regular basis. Recipes from the Byzantine and Post Byzantine period have even been discovered. Olive oil does not seem to have been used so systematically for human consumption in the other Mediterranean countries at that time.

THE CRETAN OLIVE GROVE

From the third millennium B.C., Crete was an olive oil producing area. Since the climatic conditions of the island are ideal for the growth of the tree, the people   turned their interest to the cultivation of olive trees, which was easy and profitable. The Cretans have never stopped

An olive tree in Athens during the Turkish rule.

A centuries-old olive grove.

cultivating their beloved tree. Even when other areas developed, such as Athens, and the island's trade declined, Crete continued to produce large quantities of olive oil. It was used for food, as a manufacturing material in the production of scented oil and as an industrial material on its own. It was olive oil which lit public and private buildings.

During the 5th and 4th centuries B.C., olive oil became the island's most important product for export on the Egyptian market. In the years that followed, there was a decline in olive cultivation which was probably due to the great demand for the renowned Cretan wine. Crete was en-slaved by the Arabian–Saracens who came from Spain between 828 and 961 A.D. The island was freed and became a Byzantine district which was subdued by the Jesuits in 1204. The latter sold the island to the Venetians in 1211 and from then on until 1669, it was under Venetian occupation. It was then that the Turks gained control of Crete and they stayed on the island until 1898. Since then, Crete has been free. An increase in the cultivation of olive trees seems to have started towards the end of the 16th century. Throughout the following centuries, the making of soap developed so much that Cretan olive oil became a coveted product.

The Turkish occupation made conditions difficult on the island. The rural population endured harsh tax laws and a variety of other problems, but the

Cretan farming community managed to survive due to the productive nature of the land. Some of the basic agricultural products, among which is olive oil, were never in short supply for the majority of the farmers' households. The production of olive oil tripled from the beginning to the end of the 18th century! This increase in the production has continued since then.

OLIVE OIL SOAP

Seals used for stamping soap. They belong to the authors' private collection.

✳ As time passed by, the French continued to buy large amounts of olive oil for the increased demand of the soap industry. At the same time, local businesses were set up in Greece. Having the pure product at hand, some people started, although rather tentatively at first, to develop a business which was to become an important industrial and economic occupation for the country for almost two hundred years, until the beginning of the 20th century.

There were such groups to be found in the Cretan towns.

Even today, a high quality white or green soap made from olive oil is still produced.

OLIVE OIL AS FOOD

"Olive oil in Greece takes the place butter has in the English diet"
(Antony Andrews, "Ancient Greek Society")

Olive oil had been essential for lighting as well as a basic dietary requirement since prehistoric times. Its uses in cooking were extended during the classical period. Complicated forms of cooking were concocted in order to meet the demand for unusual ideas. Archestratus has informed us about some rather interesting recipes using fish; olive oil was often used with cheese and vegetables. Two-banded bream for example, a well known tasty fish, was cooked with cheese and olive oil. Glaucus (a kind of sea bass) was boiled in water with spices and olive oil. Then the fish was put in brine. This is all according to the recipe which was saved by Oreibasius, a famous doctor in the Byzantine times.

Olive oil was essential in cooking cereal crops, vegetables and pulses as it still is today in traditional Greek cuisine, especially in the areas where olive trees are abundant. Olive oil which is to be used for cooking purposes is always of a very high standard, obviously depending on the conditions of production in every area. Farmers were used to consuming the olive oil without it being cooked, which is not such an unusual occurrence even today, either by pouring the oil on a traditional Greek dried rusk or by flavouring boiled greens and other kinds of salad. The amounts of uncooked oil that were consumed were not small. Olive oil was not only used for basic cooking, but also for making sweets. Athenaeus, a great writer who recorded a lot of information about food and diet in the Roman era, mentions an ancient Cretan sweet which was called "glycinas". It was made *"with sweet wine and olive oil"*. Many sweets in ancient times and even today's traditional ones rely on olive oil.

Wine, wheat, olive oil...

In the Christian religion, olive oil achieved a greater level of importance in that it is one of the three blessed products:

"...To mankind who is a civilized animal and honoured by the great god, excellent food, bread, wine and olive oil, was given. The bread supports and strengthens the heart, the wine lightens the spirit and the oil relaxes the body in that it cures and alleviates demanding hardships. It was God, like a father, who gave these things so that there was a rich table of offerings", says Eusevius, the religious writer, around 335 A.D.

In the Byzantine period, olive oil was accessible to a large proportion of the population. It was certainly not absent from the tables of the emperors and the urban classes nor from the tables of the abbots and monks in the monasteries and of course it was not missing from the tables of the poor farmers. Olive oil was used in many complicated recipes that were specially designed for the Emperor's table. Byzantine chefs discovered amazing ways of using the product. It seems that in Constantinople in the Middle Ages, cooking had reached a very high level for that period. It should also not be forgotten that forks appeared for the first time at Byzantine tables and were transported to the West around the 10th century when Theodora Douka married in Venice, as forks were part of her dowry!

Olive oil, wheat and wine in the Sacrament of Holy Unction.

Olive oil was brought into the range of special religious foods that were forbidden during celebrations in the Orthodox calendar. During fasting, the consumption of animal products and olive oil is not allowed. The common classes of the empire ensured that on the other days their daily intake included vegetables, cereals and pulses. Olive oil played an important role in the making of simple yet satisfying dishes. The "holy juice" was vividly described by Ptochoprodromos, a hungry monk who left us with valuable accounts of his time, as a plain onion soup which was seasoned with herbs

The "mistato".
A jar used for
measuring
olive oil.

and olive oil. This was eaten with pieces of bread which were dunked in the soup. During the 17th century, when Greece was almost entirely under Turkish control, olive oil continued to be thought of as *"a great gift that cured everything in life".* This same idea was used in Byzantium in the 9th century A. D. but it is slightly different: *"it is fattening and gives strength or, in other words, it does only good and no harm at all to those who consume it"!* That is what Agapios Landos, a Cretan monk from Aghion Oros (Mount Athos) said.

For the farming families in the Middle Ages, olive oil was an easy and suitable solution and so it continued to be in subsequent years. On Crete, even in the middle of the 20th century, a little olive oil on a traditional dried rusk with salt and oregano could take the place of a meal.

Cretan people. The studies show that they enjoy the best health and that they consume the greatest amount of olive oil in the world!

OLIVE OIL IN THE CRETAN DIET. THE STUDY OF THE SEVEN COUNTRIES

"Olives and olive oil play an important role in the Cretan diet. A foreign visitor has the impression that Cretan food literally floats in olive oil"

(Experimental research by the Rockefeller Foundation, 1948).

"They even cook pork in olive oil"

(M. Chourmouzis – Vyzantius, 1842)

※ Today, the Cretan diet is believed to be the best example of a Mediterranean diet and researchers have discovered that the Cretans have the lowest rate of heart diseases and cancer. The Cretans' good health is thought to be due to their diet. The largest role in the Cretan diet is played by olive oil.

The surprise felt by travellers when they saw Cretans or inhabitants from other large olive growing areas consuming oil unsparingly is quite justi-

fied. These habits were completely different from their own dietary ideas. Animal fat is the norm in the urban communities of central Europe. The English traveller Robert Pashley, who toured Crete shortly after the revolution of 1821 (the rebellion which brought about freedom for only one part of Greece), has provided us with important pictures of everyday life, which in themselves prove the leading role of olive oil in the diet of the inhabitants. In the villages he was often offered boiled artichokes with a lot of olive oil, eggs and wonderful wine, or greens with olive oil. Observing carefully, he calculated that each Cretan family consumed four okades (1 oka = 1280 grams) of oil every week, in other words, more than 350 litres a year! The Cretans, he says, *are learned in olive oil*. They give it to their children on bread, they use it with all greens, even with meat and fish. "It is the only thing that they are liberal with", he notes! The extreme consumption of olive oil made a lasting impression on all visitors to the olive producing areas of Greece during the 19th century. M. Chourmouzis – Vyzantius fought against the Turkish occupation of Crete in the years 1828-1829 and subsequently lived on the island for six years in total. He keenly observed the habits of the local population. The extensive use of olive oil was what impressed him most. He says that the Cretans *"ate vegetables as well as different types of tasty wild greens which, along with barley bread, are very good for them"*. He says that the inhabitants of the island overused olive oil and notes with surprise, *"they cook even pork in olive oil"*. The observations made by Chourmouzis-Vyzantius had previously been made by many others who had visited the oil producing areas of Greece, such as Pouqueville and Bartholdy.

Even in Constantinople where Chourmouzis-Vyzantius gained his experiences, the cuisine had different styles. The study of the Seven Countries which was organized by Anzel Keys towards the end of the 1950s greatly surprised the international scientific community. The Cretans, whose food floated in oil, were found to have the best health in the world. Cancerous diseases

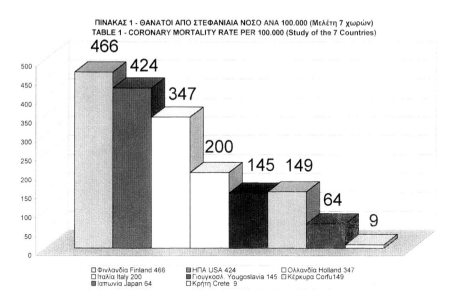

ΠΙΝΑΚΑΣ 1 - ΘΑΝΑΤΟΙ ΑΠΟ ΣΤΕΦΑΝΙΑΙΑ ΝΟΣΟ ΑΝΑ 100.000 (Μελέτη 7 χωρών)
TABLE 1 - CORONARY MORTALITY RATE PER 100.000 (Study of the 7 Countries)

□ Φινλανδία Finland 466   ■ ΗΠΑ USA 424   □ Ολλανδία Holland 347
□ Ιταλία Italy 200   ■ Γιουγκοσλ. Yougoslavia 145   □ Κέρκυρα Corfu149
■ Ιαπωνία Japan 64   □ Κρήτη Crete 9

DEATHS FROM CORONARY DISEASE PER 100,000 INHABITANTS (study of the 7 countries)

were rare, in fact much less frequent than all the areas studied and perhaps in all the world, and cardiovascular diseases (a real threat for inhabitants in the north), were almost unknown on Crete. Keys himself bore witness to the fact that the Cretans consumed large amounts of olive oil: *"You should see how much olive oil they use"!*

A few years earlier on Crete, an experimental survey was carried out on the society and economy of the island by the American Rockefeller Foundation (L. G. Allbaugh-G. Soule). The chapter about diet contains a lot of information about the island. Let us look at one observation in the study:

"Olives and olive oil make up a large part of the Cretan diet. A foreign visitor has the impression that Cretan food floats in oil. This product is unsparingly used in cooking. It is essential for salads, soups and vegetables..."

In another part it states:

"The consumption of fat, but most importantly of all, olive oil is great. This level of olive oil consumption is characteristic of the Cretan diet, in fact, much greater than anywhere else in Greece".

Any other form of fat would only occasionally be used on Crete.

THE CONSUMPTION OF OLIVE OIL
IN THE CRETAN DIET

The study of the seven countries in the 1950s showed that the consumption of olive oil on Crete was extremely high in comparison to the other areas of the Mediterranean and especially in contrast to the northern countries. In

reality, the consumption of fat by the Cretans, the other Mediterranean countries, Holland and the U.S.A. is shown as being 95, 60, 79 and 33 grams per person per day accordingly. On Crete and in the other Mediterranean countries the fat is almost entirely olive oil whereas in the U.S.A., it is other kinds of oils. In Holland, butter and animal fats are the norm. Similar studies by Eurostat, the statistics service of the European Union, showed that, in 1996, the consumption of olive oil was at a level of 31 litres annually per person on Crete, 25 litres in the other Mediterranean countries and only 185 grams per person per year in Germany!

These rates of consumption show 85 and 62 grams per person per day for the two population groups, further emphasizing an important stability in the use of olive oil, despite the great social and dietary changes which have taken place in all the Mediterranean countries in the last few decades.

THE USE OF OLIVE OIL
FOR LIGHTING

Since prehistoric times olive oil has been used for the lighting of houses and public buildings.

The use of olive oil as lighting material has created a range of symbols in that olive oil is seen as a source of light!

In evening ceremonies which required lighting, the role of olive oil was sacred, as it still is in today's worship. According to Herodotus (5th century B.C.) there was a special celebration in Egypt which was known as

A lit oil lamp hanging in front of Christ's icon.

Olive oil is the most ancient source of lighting. An oil lamp which was in use up until the middle of 20th century.

A bronze oil lamp from the town of Archanes, dated back to the Roman period.

"lychnokajia" (lighting of the lamps). All people lit their lamps and it was a spectacular event.
In Byzantine times, olive oil was essential for the "lychnokajia" in the monasteries and the churches.
Up until the first few decades of this century, the farming population of Greece had olive oil as their basic fuel for lighting.

THE OLIVE AND ITS OIL AS A MEDICINE

Bathing and rubbing with olive oil during the Olympic and other games in Greek ancient times.

A writer in ancient times known as Aelianus (3rd century AD), claimed that olive oil and the olive tree flowers were medicines that could be used even on elephants so as to pull out arrows if hunters had succeeded in hitting them:

"When an elephant is injured by many arrow heads, it eats olive tree flowers or oil and then whatever has hurt it can be removed. It is at once again strong".

It is well known that olive oil was believed to be a cure for all wounds and this knowledge continued in folklore medicine for many centuries.

Doctors in ancient times and in the Byzantine world mention an array of prescriptions which use olive oil as a basic ingredient. It was mainly used against fever by being rubbed onto the body of the person who had a temperature and also as a neurological medicine. Many doctors in ancient times recommended bathing in lukewarm olive oil for those who suffered from neuralgia.

There are many ancient prescriptions which use olive oil as a basic ingredient. In general we could say that there were hardly any illnesses that could not be cured with olive oil. It was used against poisoning, for oral health and in keeping teeth white, against stomach problems, dermatitis and leprosy which was a disease that continually appeared in the sub-tropical areas up until quite recently. The best oil for therapeutic reasons was the oil taken from the oil lamps of the icons.

Fr. Richard, who visited the island of Chios in 1650, wrote that the abbot of the New Monastery, gave out threads, which had been dipped in the oil of these lamps, to the faithful!

OLIVE OIL AS AN APHRODISIAC

"Eat olive oil and come at night
eat butter and sleep tight"

✳ Folklore medicine used olive oil as an aphrodisiac. The saying repeated in many olive oil producing areas of Greece is *"eat olive oil and come at night"* and this echoes folklore ideas. On Crete, olive oil which had not been cooked was deemed to be a much more effective aphrodisiac, especially if the oil came from the wild varieties of olive trees.

It was with this belief that many newly weds had to eat bread soaked in the first olive oil of the year. It was thought to be an elixir for conception in the south of Crete. A Thessalian saying judges the fat content of the oil and believes it is an aphrodisiac (a belief that is held all over Greece) and that butter is a substance which weakens the sexual desire:

"Eat butter and sleep tight
eat olive oil and come at night"

THE OLIVE AND ITS OIL IN WORSHIP

Tree culture. The growth of the olive tree and its symbolism in eternal life

The olive tree impressed prehistoric man because it lived for hundreds of years and almost never dried out! New shoots grew in the dried trunks and so the plant was reborn. In the prehistoric religions of the Eastern Mediterranean, man worshipped an immortal couple, a goddess who is today known as the "Great Mother" and a young god who died and was reborn every year, along with the growth of plants. This brought about the creation of a religious tradition of respect towards nature. Evidence from Neolithic Crete has led us to the conclusion that man worshipped certain trees. They acted out dances of worship under these trees and touched them as maybe they wished to draw strength from them. Some of these trees seem to have been olive trees. The first piece of evidence regarding the

special role which the olive tree played in worship can be seen on the sarcophagus at Aghia Triatha which was found in Messara on Crete. The tree can be recognized in the sacred grove, behind the altar.

In ancient Athens (around 5th century B.C. or even earlier) an olive tree was worshipped which was to be found on the rock of the Acropolis. It is said that it was planted by the bright ancient goddess Athena, who was the beloved daughter of Zeus and herself the goddess of wisdom.

The custom of worshipping sacred trees continued for thousands of years in the Greek region.

Olive branches and leaves in burial customs

There are many forms of evidence from ancient times which show that olive branches and leaves were put in graves and it was not unusual to place

An olive tree next to an Orthodox church.

Representation of a sacred tree of worship on a Minoan ring from Archanes.

A wild olive tree on a steep slope. Aghiopharago (Holy Gorge), Crete.

the body of the dead person on a layer of olive branches. Perhaps it was believed that the contact with the leaves of the immortal tree would bring the body closer to everlasting life. In graves from the 5th and 6th centuries B.C., remnants of the olive leaves on which the dead person was placed, have been found in the area of Pherae. At Sparta, the great law-maker, Lykourgos, who lived around 800 B.C., forced people to bury the dead on olive branches! This is stated by Plutarchus (46-127 A.D.) in his biography of the leader. The amazing survival of ancient burial customs must be a tradition which was recorded in the village of Petrokefali in Heraklion on Crete, where it is still practised today. The priest is the one who cuts olive branches (usually three) and at the end of the burial ceremony, just before the grave is closed, he throws them on top of the coffin.

Olive trees at graves

In ancient times it was not unusual to plant olive trees next to graves as well as other trees, such as cypress trees.

Holy olive tree

In later burial traditions, the planting of trees went in hand with the hope of rebirth. At Asterousia on Crete, an area with vivid memories of the anchorites who lived there until the beginning of 20th century, there was, till recently, a custom which strongly recalls those of ancient times. A branch from an olive tree was usually placed next to the graves of the hermits. This stayed there, normally on the eastern side of the grave and in some cases it took root and started to grow. This growth of an olive branch was a sign of holiness for whoever lay in the grave.

Olive Tree and Purification "Iketiria" (Supplication)

The olive tree was used in ancient times as a basic material of purification. Suppliants fled to holy places of worship with olive branches in their hand. In other words, whoever had committed a murder or some other extremely serious crime or injustice looked for mercy in the temples of the gods. The sup-

The olive trees next to churches preserve memories from old worship customs.

pliant begged for asylum from the holy altars, knowing that nobody could touch him there.

The suppliant, usually weighed down by the terrible crime of murder, fled to the temples of the gods, holding the "iketiria", an olive branch, on the top of which sheep's wool, normally white, had been wound. He would leave the olive branch, his supplication, on the altar and stay there so as to avoid the wrath of the relations of the person he had killed who would obviously want to take revenge. The branch would remain on the altar for as long as the supplication took. When the town authorities agreed to the suppliant's plea for mercy, only then could that person remove the olive branch from the altar and leave. He would then usually be tried in some sort of court.

In sacrifice processions, we see the worshippers making their way towards the holy altar holding branches, which are most probably olive tree branches. With the passing of time, the tradition of suppliants going to holy places holding olive branches can be seen clearly in the Greek and the Roman world.

"Eiresioni". Ancient Harvest Celebrations

During the celebration of the harvest in ancient times, an olive tree branch in blossom was offered to the gods (and sometimes laurel ones) from which hung many fruit, sheep's wool and small flasks which contained olive oil, honey and wine. This was known as "eiresioni". It was a show of gratitude to the gods for the bountiful earth which had given mankind the essential products to survive on.

Modern Greeks use olive branches on the first day of the year in the hope of a good harvest. In northern areas, sprigs from olive trees are placed in icon bases along with the wish: *"A good year has come, let the bad year leave"*.

SYMBOLIZATION
The tree of peace

The use of olive branches in a range of ancient rituals, such as in purification, shows clearly how the olive tree was a sign of goodness. The same tree was linked to light since the burning of olive oil was the leading source of light. This consolidation of ideas which is almost the same in all Mediterranean civilizations, gave a specific position to the olive tree. The olive tree is the tree of hope in the Old Testament but also a tree a message of mercy from God, that was brought to the arc by a dove to show that the flood had ended.

Greek tradition looks upon this tree as the symbol of peace. Eirini (Peace) herself, the goddess who was the daughter of Zeus and Themis, is pictured with an olive branch in her hands. There was no better way or symbol of the end of a war than a branch from this tree. Messengers who were sent with a message of peace or to ask for a settlement, carried an olive branch in their hands. It was the unquestioned holy symbol which declared the intentions of those who decided to send it.

OLIVE OIL IN BURIAL CEREMONIES

From prehistoric times, the two most valuable liquids in the Mediterranean seem to have had their own particular roles in the ceremonies for the dead. In prehistoric graveyards, there are establishments for the pressing of grapes and possibly olives. Libations of oil were often made to the graves in ancient times. Even today on Crete, the first way of caring for the dead is the making of a cross on the chest and back of the dead person. The mixture that is used is a blend of oil and wine.

Even today in Orthodox worship, the priest, at the grave side, sprinkles the dead person with olive oil from the oil lamps of the icons.

MEDICINE FOR BOTH THE SOUL AND THE BODY. THE CHRISTIAN PERCEPTION

Olive oil heals wounds and so it can help in the relief of daily stresses and the burden of sins or actions which go against a Christian way of life. Marcus the Evangelist informed us that Christ's disciples annointed sick people with olive oil and so cured them.

The basic idea that olive oil is a means of treating wounds and other bodily ailments, is not far from the well-known use of it in the ancient world. To those Christianity added diseases of the soul and mind.

An interesting ritual which treated illnesses, took place in the worship of the Pagans. At the circle of Apollonius Tyaneus, a philosopher whose followers worshipped him like a god, especially in 3rd century AD, it seems that a mysterious evening ritual took place whereby, *"in the seventh hour of the night"* water was taken and mixed with oil which was then annointed on the *"sleepless patient"* who was then immediately cured.

BAPTISM

In the baptism ceremony, olive oil is the way in which the grace of God is transferred to the newly baptized member of the church. According to Christian faith, the baptism symbolizes both death and rebirth.

Purification is carried out with the use of the water which was the basic liquid of cleansing even in ancient worship, and in which drops of olive oil and wine had been poured crosswise. The baptized person is reborn, free from the weight of the in-

The olive oil after the baptirm calms the sea.

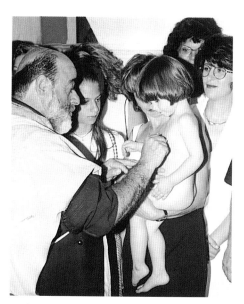

"Olive oil seal" in the sacrament of baptism.

herited original sin and prepared for the third birth, eternal life. For this reason, the baptized person wears new clothes. The baptism ceremony starts with the annointing of the body of the person who is to be baptized with purifying oil. The priest "seals" the body three times and reads the benediction of olive oil. Then he dips his finger in the oil and annoints the person to be baptized in the form of crosses on the forehead, the chest and on the back, imbetween the shoulder blades. The ceremony is then completed with the dipping of the person in the water which is essential as this holy olive oil stands as a seal of the newly baptized Christian. The new member of the church can only then formerly enter with the seal of God.

HARVEST CELEBRATIONS

The olive harvest is a celebration in Greece. Until a few years ago, there was a feast at the end of the gathering. This was to be seen in many oil producing areas. In eastern Crete, namely Sitia, "apomazochtikia" survived up until the 20th century. This was a special celebration which took place once the harvesting had finished. Housewives prepared a celebration in the home where relatives joined in, along with friends and the workers who did the gathering of the olives. Food was made with the newly harvested oil, even if there was still some left from the year before. The appropriate bread was baked, the chick pea bread, (eftazymo), and the table was covered with lots of food so that the year would be one of great bounty. The special sweet for this occasion was the olive oil pie, which was a pie made with grape juice syrup and offered at the end of the dinner. Such celebrations took place on the islands in the Aegean and the Ionian Sea.

OLIVE OIL CALMS THE SEA

On the islands of the Aegean, on Crete and in other sea-bordered areas, the oil from Saint Nikolas' oil lamp is kept, the saint who protects sailors. When the sea blows a storm, a few drops of the oil are poured into the water. This immediately calms the sea.

THE OLIVE TREE ON PALM SUNDAY

It is quite usual even today, on Palm Sunday, for a branch from an olive tree to be taken to the church by a faithful worshipper.

These days, a branch is taken to the church in the afternoon on the Saturday before Holy Week, where it stays all night. When the time comes for the procession of the icons around the church, two youths take the branch and lead the priests and the worshippers. This holy procession goes around the church three times and ends in an open area, usually outside the entrance of the church. In front of the branch, the Gospel is read while at the same time, hands reach up to touch it. When the phrase "others cut branches from the trees" is heard, the worshippers snap off a piece of the branch and take it home with them. These pieces are placed on icons in homes and are considered to be protection against various illnesses. On Crete, patients and even sick animals are adorned with these pieces from the olive tree branch.

This tradition has been in practice since at least 1674. A traveller of that time saw it in a church in Constantinople and wrote: *"the Christians placed a large branch from an olive tree in every church"*.

THE OLIVE AND ITS OIL IN ANCIENT MYTHOLOGY

ATHENS 2004

The olive branch wreath which has been chosen to be the sign of the Olympic games in 2004 in Athens.

THE CRETAN WILD OLIVE TREE IN OLYMPIA

Representations from ancient games.

The deified worshipping parties of Crete, the Kouretes and the Idaean Dactyls, were those who brought the olive to the Greek area. In the Roman period, these holy demons were believed by the Cretans to be great providers of mankind. They were believed to have developed arts and various artifacts, metallurgy, medicine, bee keeping, herding, hunting weapons, such as the bow and arrow, ceremonial dances and the drum, to mention but a few. One of these Kouretes who was called Heracles (not the famed one of Greek mythology) first planted the wild olive tree in Olympia. He was the founder of the Olympic games. According to ancient sources, the Cretan Heracles brought the olive tree from the north or from his homeland, Crete.

The Idaean Heracles had four brothers, Paeoneus, Epimides, Iasius and Idas. He was the oldest brother and one day he took his siblings to Olympia to run. It was the first race in the world! Heracles awarded the winner with a branch from the olive tree which he himself had planted there. So the custom of awarding the winner with a garland started, one made from a wild olive tree. This custom was retained in ancient times and was seen as an impressive symbol. In ancient times, the garland made from an olive branch was...

"the most beautiful commemoration of
those who won the races at Olympia..."

ELAIS, SPERMO AND OINO

✳ Elais, Spermo and Oino were the daughters of Anios who in turn was the child of Dionysus and Ariadne. In Greek, their names relate to the three main products of the Greek land: Elais (olive), Spermo (wheat, cereals) and Oino (wine).

They were Anios' daughters and Dionysus' granddaughters and were born on a small island in the Aegean known as Delos. Their grandfather, Dionysus, gave them a special gift, to have olive oil, wheat and wine whenever they wanted.

ATHENA'S GIFT OF THE OLIVE TREE

✳ The most well known ancient myth relating to the cultivation of the olive tree tells how Athena, the great goddess, gave the olive tree as a present. Some state that she first planted the tree on Crete and later in Athens whereas others believe that the wise goddess first planted this tree on the holy rock of the Acropolis.

It all started with the disagreement between Athena and Poseidon. Athena was the goddess of wisdom and Poseidon was the god of the sea. Both of them wanted to govern Athens, the most amazing Greek city in the classical period.

Based on this, each immortal decided to offer an invaluable present. The winner of this unusual contest was to be the one who offered the most precious gift. The judges of these two gods were all the other immortals who did not take pleasure in watching this contest between the gods. Poseidon, lord of the seas, appeared in the contest with his trident, the one which decided the fate of the seas. He lifted his trident and stabbed it into the side of the holy rock of the Acropolis. Salty water started to fall down the sides of the rock. It has been said that he opened a well with his trident on the rock of the Acropolis and that it was full of salty water. Poseidon believed that such a well in Attica would bring him victory. Athena did not need to do anything too impressive. She bent down and planted an olive tree in the same spot. Others suggest that she did not plant it herself. She just stabbed her javelin into the earth and the tree immediately flourished. Its silver-green foliage impressed everyone. That was it! The world had never seen such a tree. As people could not try cooked food or enjoy a lit night as there was no suitable fuel for the wicks, the gods judged that Athena's gift was of invaluable worth.

The holy tree of Athens has a story of its own in the city. In 480 B.C., when the Persians invaded and took the Acropolis, the holy tree of Athena was burned down, much to the great sadness of the Athenians who took it to be a very bad sign. This despair turned to joy the next morning when from the burnt remains of the tree, appeared a new bud. This young plant was the new holy tree of Athena's!

Ancient Athenian coins with an olive branch wreath and an olive branch accordingly.

THE OLIVE TREE
AND
ALIRROTHIOS

※ The decision of the gods which sided with Athena in the battle over Athens, greatly angered Poseidon, who as ruler of the seas, never allowed Attica to have enough water. Not only was Poseidon upset by this

The Acropolis of Athens.

decision but also his family. One of his sons, an offspring from his affair with the nymph Euryte, was called Alirrothios. Angered by the lack of respect shown to his father, Alirrothios went up to the top of the holy rock of the Acropolis, took an axe and tried to chop down the one and only olive tree which Athena had planted. The axe slipped in his hands so that, instead of hitting the olive tree, it stuck him and cut off his head or his leg, but the result was his death.

AN OLIVE TREE
FROM
HERACLES' CLUB

Heracles, the renowned hero of Greek mythology, always held a club with which he faced all dangers and came out as a winner. He had cut it from a large wild olive tree which he had found near the Saronic Gulf, close to Athens. Once, Heracles went to the city of Troezena in the Peloponnese and found himself in front of the statue of Hermes, the young messenger of the gods. Heracles touched the statue of Hermes with his club and the club suddenly grew leaves and roots.

When the great traveller Pausanias went to Troezena, he was shown a wild olive tree growing next to the statue of Hermes and was told that it was the tree which had grown from the dried club of the mythical hero.

LATER MYTHS AND TRADITIONS ABOUT THE OLIVE TREE

Centuries-old olive trees with their enormous dry trunks were the reason for a moral telling myth which explained why the olive tree always had a dried heart.

When Christ was crucified and sadness spread throughout the world, the leaves of the trees fell down and the rocks split in two. Only the olive tree stayed as it was and none of its leaves fell off. The other trees were disturbed by this and so asked why this was so. The olive tree answered, *"your leaves have fallen but they will re-grow. My leaves did not fall but my heart knows only too well"*. That is why the core or heart of an olive tree is always dry...

THE TEARS OF CHRIST

Cretan folklore tradition which describes the uniqueness of olive oil, links it with the tears of Christ:

"At the time when they hunted, caught and crucified Christ, he was in a great depression. He looked for peace but could not find it as his enemies were in close pursuit. He eventually reached an olive tree where he sat down under its shade and lay his head on its trunk so as to rest for a while. But he found it impossible to sleep. Filled with sadness, he burst into tears. His tears fell to the ground and watered the roots of the tree. The olive tree is a blessed plant, having been watered by Christ, and so it is for this reason that it gives oil, the most delicious ingredient of foods, which gives light to the lamps in churches and monasteries. There is no other more blessed tree in the world, for what other tree can boast of having drunk the warm tears of Christ himself?"

OLIVES AS A FOOD

E ven in prehistoric times, the olive was well known as a food. In the beginning there was not the knowledge regarding the processing or the soaking of olives. It was natural in early societies for the olive to be seen as a seasonal type of food. In other words, olives were only consumed during the period when they ripened and became edible. So it follows that those olives consumed, were the ones that ripened on the trees naturally. With the passing of time, the inhabitants of the Mediterranean areas who looked upon the olive as an essential part of their diet, developed various methods of keeping olives for a long period of time after the point of harvesting. Several forms of soaking and preservation were developed. For many centuries, a basic ingredient used in the preservation

of olives was salt and as additional ingredients they used honey, olive oil, vinegar and vine juice (which could easily be made into wine and wine in turn could be made into vinegar). Aromatic plants were used as preservers but also as a way of improving the flavour of the oil.

Ancient techniques of soaking the bitterness out of the olives survived for many centuries. Some of these methods are still used today! The farming population has hardly modernized the production of edible olives.

For many years, the olive remained a food stuff of the farming communities, nomads, travellers and the army. Apart from being food of the farming classes, olives were one of the most important appetizers in the ancient world. For this reason, olives were also used on patients as a form of therapy, especially in cases which showed symptoms of lack of appetite. Olives were the favourite starter of the Romans. They were served as a starter at the beginning of a meal at a rich symposium. But as they were loved so much and the greed at Roman symposiums knew no limit, olives were also served for dessert! Lunch or dinner started and ended with olives!

Greek varieties of edible olives

OLIVES IN THE FASTING OF THE ORTHODOX CHURCH

The Orthodox Church requires bodily cleansing prior to big holidays, such as Christmas, Easter and 15th August. Such demands are also made whereby fasting is required on other days in monasteries, on Wednesdays and Fridays. On these days, animal based products are forbidden. Big feasts even disallow the consumption of olive oil but not the olives themselves.

The use of the olive as an allowed food product during times of fasting has proved to be invaluable for long periods of the year. For this reason, monasteries have developed production techniques and consider the olives, like wine and wheat (bread), to be the items which should never be missing from the cellars of a monastery. Pierre Bellon who travelled through Greece in 16th century noted that the basic food of the monks on Mount Athos was salted olives, broad beans and greens. The great Cretan writer Nikos Kazantzakis described the lives of the hermits who lived in the caves: *"A basket is hung near the sea and when a boat passes by, a little bread and some olives are thrown in ... ... so as not to leave the hermits to die of hunger..."*

TRADITIONAL GREEK VARIETIES

※ In Greece, there is a long tradition in the production of the ripe black olive, of which there are many varieties, in comparison to other olive cultivating countries, such as Spain where they concentrate on the green olive. The easiest and most natural olive to be consumed by man was the throumba or stafidolia, in other words, a ripe olive which loses its bitterness on its own with natural processes on the tree. But there are other types of olives such as the charaktes (slit) ones and those in vinegar or oil or brine which are still favourites of Greeks. In many Greek areas, soaking techniques for green olives have been known for a long time.

Types of olives depend on their final usage. There are some olives which are only for eating whereas others are for oil making. Many regions in Greece cultivate olives which can be used for both. As some large olives do not provide a good quality of oil, Greek farmers separate their crops, in order to produce good quality harvests.

GREEK TABLE OLIVES

Konservolia

※ This is the most famous Greek variety of table olives. It makes up about 80% of table olive production in Greece. This variety is grown in central Greece and is known by the name of the area producing it, that is, olives of Amfissa, Agrinion, Volos, Atalanti, Aghios Konstantinos, Stylida etc. The fruits are of medium to large size (weighing between 5 and 8 or even 12 grams). They are round to oval and are preserved in brine.

Nychati of Kalamata

※ This is one of the most important Greek table olive varieties. It is produced in the south and south-western region of the Peloponnese and particularly in Messinia and Laconia as well as in central Greece. The fruit is of medium size (3-6 grams). They are black olives and their oil content is 25%. They are used for the preparation of slit olives preserved in brine and vinegar.

Olives of Chalkidiki

※ In the last few years, it has become known as a very important variety of table olives. It comes from the peninsula of Chalkidiki, close to Mount Athos. Its fruit is very large and for this reason the variety is known as "gaidourolia" (donkey olive).

Megaritiki

※ This is a dual-purpose variety, used for both oil production and eating. It is cultivated in the region of Attica. Its fruit is small and used mainly for the preparation of black dry-salted olives or of green cracked (tsakistes) olives.

Kothreiki

※ This is a dual-purpose variety, produced in the Greek Mainland. Its fruit is similar in colour and shape to the fruit of the konservolia variety.

Karydolia

※ It is considered to be a clone of the konservolia variety and is grown in the region of Euboea.

Olives of Egumenitsa

This, too, is considered to be a clone of the konservolia variety producing a fruit of smaller size and grown in the area of Egumenitsa (Epirus).

Throumba, throumbolia

The fruit of this variety is of small to medium size and loses its bitterness and becomes sweet on the tree during ripening. The tree thrives on Crete, the Aegean islands or the region of Attica. The loss of bitterness is due to the activity of a fungus growing on the skin of the olive fruit. This variety is used for the production of throumba black olives (see below).

Stafidolies (throumba olives). An excellent produce!

The stafidolies (wrinkled olives) or throumba olives are very special and important edible olives, very close to the present dietary requirements, as they are edible without the addition of much salt. The fruit is a natural product needing no processing to lose its bitterness. The olives mature on the tree and it is from there they are picked manually. Lately the harvesting method has become simpler. Wide nets are spread out under the trees, the olives are knocked down onto them and are collected from there more easily. Then they are washed thoroughly, spread outdoors to dry and finally they are packed under a vacuum with the addition of a small quantity of solid salt to improve their taste. They can alternatively be packed into containers filled with good quality olive oil, without salt. These days they are preserved for months in the freezer without any salt. They should be taken out of the freezer a few minutes before they are consumed.

These olives are wrinkled and probably for this reason many people do not like them. Nevertheless, the conscious consumers do not take this "disadvantage" into consideration, as their advantages from the nutritional point of view are so many.

Modern views for less salt in the diet can be a serious reason for the propagation of this absolutely natural and healthy product.

Other Greek table olive varieties

There are some more Greek varieties of table olives which are not available on the market today. You can discover olives of excellent quality throughout Greece (such as the cracked olives known from even antiquity, or the kolymbathes, which have a long history themselves). You can try the small Cretan olives prepared from the "tsounati" variety, olives flavoured with herbs, bitter orange, orange etc., olives preserved in olive oil and many others. Unfortunately, they are not all available on the market.

PROCESSING OF TABLE OLIVES

※ The methods of curing edible olives at home vary, but they are all based on the techniques known from ancient times. For the varieties which do not mature on the tree, the traditional processing requires soaking in water with salt or ashes. Slitting the olive lengthwise with a sharp knife as well as cracking the flesh open, usually with a wooden object, being careful not to touch the pit, are methods used even today in many Greek areas. This procedure varies depending on the type of olives and how ripe they are. The traditional methods of curing edible olives have been modernized and give excellent natural products.

HOW TO MAKE YOUR OWN TABLE OLIVES!

Kalamata slit olives in olive oil.

※ If you can find black olives of the Kalamata variety, try this traditional recipe.

These olive fruits are large and are gathered when they are deep black but before they are wrinkled. Select firm and unbruised olives. Incise the olives lengthwise in two places with a sharp knife without touching the stone. Place them into a large clay or plastic vase with enough water to cover them for about 12 days changing the water daily until they are no longer bitter. Prepare brine with 1 litre water and 100 grams salt for every kilo of olives, put the sweetened olives in the brine and leave them for two days. Then drain them and soak in vinegar where you have added a little water (4 parts of vinegar to 1 part of water) for another two days. Finally drain them again and store in glass or clay jars covered with olive oil. Season with bay leaves or oregano, if desired.

According to another method, after drawing out the bitterness, store them in brine acidified with vinegar, 3 parts of brine to 1 part of vinegar. (To prepare the brine, dissolve 100 grams of salt in a litre of water). Cover with a layer of olive oil, 1 cm thick, and seal the jars.

Green cracked olives (tsakistes)

How to make cracked (tsakistes) olives

❊ These olives are harvested as early as October, while they are still green, unripe.

Crack each olive open carefully with a wooden object (usually a hammer) trying not to crack the stone, only the flesh. Soak them in water for 10 days changing the water daily until they lose their bitterness. When they become sweet, store them in brine prepared with 1 litre of lukewarm water and 100 grams of salt for every kilo of olives. Add 3/4 cup of lemon juice and various herbs, such as oregano, coriander, fennel, slices of lemon, hot pepper etc., according to taste. Cover with a layer of olive oil, 1 cm thick.

Cracked olives should be consumed within a short period of time because they may bleach or get mouldy with the passing of time.

Serve sprinkled with coriander, chopped garlic, slices of lemon and olive oil mixed with lemon juice.

ATTENTION: *The jars in which the olives are stored should be put in a cool, dark place so that they can be kept for up to a year. They can also be kept in the fridge.*
Before using them, it is best to re-wash them in water and then drain them. They can be eaten on their own as a starter with bread or cheese, in salads, in various dishes, in bread making or even as a paste.

Olives scented with thyme

Scented olives with rosemary

Whether your own or bought, olives can be scented, depending on your preferences; with fennel, coriander, oregano, thyme, rosemary, laurel leaves, hot peppers, garlic, lemon, orange rind, etc...

- 2 cups olives
- 1 clove garlic
- 2 hot peppers
- 1 quartered lemon
- 1 tbsp rosemary
- 2 tbsps vinegar
- 1 cup olive oil

Mix olives with garlic, hot peppers, lemon and rosemary in a bowl. Beat olive oil with vinegar. Pour over the olives and make sure they are covered. These can be kept in a jar or the fridge for quite a while.

OLIVE PASTE

It was quite usual in ancient times to consume olive paste, either made from whole olives or from what was left of the olives after pressing. So the idea that olive paste is something new is quite unjustified, as it was common place in classic times and also could have quite possibly gone on, long before then. Callimachus the Cyrenaeus, who wrote in the first decades of 3rd century B.C., states clearly that olives can produce a ground mash.

Olive paste can be used in place of butter in breakfast (to spread on bread) or as an appetizer before a meal.
To make olive paste, mash the olives and scent them again, depending on your preferences, whether coriander, cumin, oregano, mint, fennel, thyme, garlic, onion, hot pepper, lemon, etc...

Olive paste with oregano

1	cup pitted black olives
2	cloves garlic (green core removed)
1	tbsp oregano
2	tbsps lemon juice
4	tbsps olive oil

Put the ingredients in a food processor to make the paste. Empty into a bowl and store in the fridge for a few days. Olive paste can be used at least 2 hours after being made as it needs time for the flavours to infuse.

Olive paste with fennel and mint

1	cup pitted black olives
2	tbsps finely chopped fennel or 1 tbsp fennel seeds, roasted and ground
1	clove garlic
2	tbsps fresh or dried mint
1	hot pepper
1	tbsp lemon or fresh orange juice
1	tbsp good quality vinegar
4	tbsps olive oil

Put in the ingredients in a blender to make a paste. Keep it in the fridge but let it stand for 2-3 hours before using it. It can be stored for a few days.

WHAT IS OLIVE OIL?

Olives are the fruits of the olive tree which is indigenous to the Mediterranean countries but also cultivated nowadays in other areas, even in America and Australia. There are many different kinds of olives. Some are used only for making oil, while others are for eating and these are usually large in size. There are also some varieties which are used for both oil and consumption. The tree blossoms in Spring (April – May) and shortly afterwards, the olive fruit start to grow. They are a bright green colour to begin with and this lasts until the point when they ripen. This point varies amongst the different types of olive but usually it is around the end of autumn.

The olive is a drupe, in other words, a fruit with a fleshy skin enclosing a stone and either circular or oval in shape. Olive oil is the natural juice of the olive, a pure product which is obtained with machinery or by natural means. The oil of the olive is found in the pericarp, the fleshy part of the fruit.

Attention:

There is a great difference between olive oil and seed oil when looking at its make-up and how it is obtained. Seed oil is produced from various seeds put through chemical procedures. Olive oil is only from the olive and is made in a totally natural way.

THE OLIVE HARVEST
AND OLIVE OIL PRODUCTION

Olive cultivation is relatively speaking, easy. It requires no specific farming care and the most difficult thing is collecting the fruit. It has been calculated that the gathering of olives takes 60% of the total cultivation costs of olives! It is a tough tree which thrives easily. It blossoms in April or May and then the olives begin to grow. From then until the end of autumn, the fruit are a vivid, green colour. As they begin to ripen, they redden, until they eventually turn black.

The harvesting of olives used to be done by hand in the old days when production was not so great. The olives were allowed to drop and then they were collected. For those olives which didn't fall, the tree was shaken or hit with a stick until they did and then the women, who usually had this tiring job, collected them and put the fruit in baskets or panniers as can be seen in ancient Greek and Byzantine pictures. This

Olive harvesting in older times on the island of Lesbos. Painting by Stratis Axiotis (from Th. Paraskevajidis' book, "the olive trees and the farmers on Lesbos").

The roots of an old olive tree. Olive trees never die! They sprout again from the root and re-grow.

method does not produce a good quality of oil. The traditional way of harvesting olives in areas of large production was the one using the stick. Special sticks were used to beat the trees so that the olives fell into special tarpaulins or nets that had been placed under the tree. In some areas with relatively small levels of production, it was customary to "pluck" the branches, in other words, to pull the olives off by hand and place the fruit in big baskets. This is probably the best method as you then do not bruise the olive, but this way would be impossible for large-scale harvesting.

Recent years have seen the appearance of some machines for harvesting purposes. These use the idea of a mechanised stick beating the tree, thus helping production to increase. There are small, plastic sticks which rotate on the machinery. They release the olives from the branches and the fruit fall down onto the prepared nets. Olives were taken to the oil press

Ancient olive press installations from the Minoan palace of Phaestos.

in large sacks in the old days. However, they lose their value if kept in these sacks for many days. It has therefore been established that olives need to be pressed one or two days after having been harvested. Nowadays, olives are transferred in plastic boxes, which do not bruise or press the fruit and are taken to the press on the same day they are collected.

OLIVE PRESSING

History

Stone base of an old oil mill from John Papadakis' private collection, Axos in Mylopotamos, Crete.

❊ Information about olive oil pressing in prehistoric times is not clear. The olive oil that was needed by each family seems to have been produced in small home environment. Olives were squashed in stone vessels and by adding water, the oil could be removed as it floated on the surface of the water.

At a later stage, people crushed olives imbetween large circular stones which rotated so that pulped olives produced oil along with the other natural juices of the fruit. Being, lighter, oil floated and was easily collected. Slowly but surely, the pressure which had been carried out by stone was replaced with machinery which had a lever. Pressing the olive pulp caused the oil to yield, along with the other juices. A picture from an oil press dating back to 6th century

B.C. which worked using levers, was found on Santorini. The lever was set in a sturdy place, such as a wall, so that on pressing it, the olive pulp was crushed, so producing the oil. As years went by, new types of presses were created which were able to crush evenly.

Until the first decades of the 20th century, the extraction of olive oil from the fruit was a difficult procedure. Olives were pressed on threshing floors where two large mill-stones were rotated. These were pulled by animals which trod around the stones. The pulp was then taken, a mixture of juices, oil and the pit, to be placed in cloth sacks. These sacks were piled up on top of each other and placed in the press. The pressure forced out the liquids (oil and water). The oil, being lighter, floated on the water and was easy to collect. The use of electricity put an end to the labour of the animals and the use of centrifugal power made the business of olive pressing much easier.

Installation of an old oil mill. It had been in use till the first decades of the 20th century.

Modern methods.
The "synolea" method.

Today, technology has created the best conditions for olive pressing and ex-

An old olive press in the monastery of Aghios Georghios at the village of Karythi, Chania.

traction of olive oil. The crushing is done by machinery. Special metal hammers mush the olives and there then follow various ways of oil extraction. Centrifugal power is one of those methods. The most recent way is the "synolea" method. First the olives are crushed and then special blades plunge quickly and steadily into the olive pulp. Olive oil drops rest on them, due to adherence, and these are collected. This technique produces an excellent product which retains its natural character. In general, this type of olive oil keeps its scent intact and is much tastier.

Drawing of an ancient olive press.

STORAGE OF OLIVE OIL

The storage of olive oil in glass bottles is an ideal solution in order to retain its natural character for several months, especially if the bottle is dark in colour. Olive oil is sensitive to light oxidation, which speeds up when its colouring substances come in contact with sunlight, room light, even light from fluorescent lamps. For this reason, if the bottle is transparent, it should be kept in a dark place. Ideal storage temperature is believed to be 10-15° Celsius.

Attention:

O live oil should not come into contact with metal, especially copper and iron. These metals speed up the process of acidic deterioration of the product. Storage is allowed only in non-oxidising metal containers.

OLIVE OIL QUALITIES

Practical advice

❋ Olive oil grading follows international quality standards according to the method of production, the level of acidity and basic organic characteristics. Special testers check the taste and smell of an oil. Taste and smell, in connection with colour, are the three areas checked by international testers in assessing the quality level of a product. Fluidity and a harmonious – balanced relationship between the characteristics of the oil, are used to form a final evaluation.

Colour

❋ Colour does not always prove the quality of an oil. A good oil can be from green to golden yellow. It can even seem cloudy if it has not settled yet. As colour is not a sure sign of quality, experts test olive oil in dark blue and not transparent glasses. The colour of the product depends on the main substances of the olive fruit that the oil has been made from. If chlorophyll is the main factor, then the oil will lean more towards the colour green. If carotene is the main substance, then the oil will be more golden yellow. Olives which are gathered at the beginning of the harvesting period, usually produce oil of a greener colour, due to the chlorophyll they contain.

Taste and smell

※ Olive oil reminiscent of the scent either of fruit or of oil fresh from pressing is believed to be excellent. This is the same with wine as testers try to pinpoint pleasant smells which remind them of other products, such as fruit, like apples or nuts, etc. The smell and taste are due to a large amount of scenting agents which give the consumer the idea of fresh fruit.

A bitter or slightly bitter taste shows that the olives used were not ripe when picked. A pleasant smell and taste can also be put down to the area in which the olives grew and the way they were cultivated. A fruit taste comes from ripe olives which have balanced characteristics. Olive oil with an unpleasant smell and taste is better avoided. Smelling soil or mould down-grade a product. It can be seen then that experience is needed for someone to safely assess an oil.

Acidity

※ The degree of acidity in olive oil indicates the oleic acid content. It is believed to be edible, according to the International Olive Oil Council, when the acidity does not exceed 3.3 degrees (content of oleic acid 3.3%). In reality, olive oil which has an acidity level of no more than one is much better. You should always read the label on an olive oil bottle to see the degree of the acidity. In Greece, there is excellent olive oil with acidity less than 0.5 degrees! The degree of acidity greatly affects the taste.

Olive oil with a higher lever of acidity makes its presence known on first tasting it as it has a pungent spicy unpleasant taste. Methods of harvesting, storage and pressing can affect the level of acidity. Organic olive oil producers transfer olives to the press, not in sacks but in boxes, which do not press or bruise the fruit. Also, producers take care to not store them more than one or two days so that the fruit is not spoilt.

Oxidization

※ Oxidization (rancidity) is one of the most important causes of spoiling olive oil. Conditions of storage (light, oxygen etc) help oxidization. This is easily spotted by a tester without scientific tests, as the taste is badly affected by oxidization. Olive oil producers can distinguish good quality from rancid olive oil, after years of experience. As they say, "the oil got rancid and smells like soil". On Crete, they identify the smell of rancid olive oil with the smell of soil. Similarly, at Kalavryta of the Peloponnese they say "the oil is not good because it nips the tongue".

Oxidization reduces or destroys the basic components in olive oil, especially those which are unique to this produce, in contrast to all the other fat substances. It can destroy the fat-soluble vitamins or the fatty acids such as linoleic and linolenic but it can also produce substances which are dangerous for the human body.

OLIVE OIL CHARACTERISTICS

These are pinpointed by testers. Try a few different kinds of olive oil. Experience will help you to choose the oil you prefer.

Organic olive oil

❈ Greek olive oil is in general, of good quality. Cultivation methods do not use a lot of fertilizers. The main chemical treatment which is carried out is spraying olive trees at random, in an attempt to combat the olive tree's worst enemy, dacus oleae. It is an olive fruit fly which destroys olive production. Farmers use chemicals which act as bait, attract the insects and eventually kill them. Natural cultivation is taken even further when you consider that without these chemicals (fertilizers, pesticides, insecticides), the farmer has to encounter a range of olive tree related diseases. In the last few years, many naturally cultivating olive producers have appeared in Greece. These farmers have made progress and have been internationally recognized.

> ### Attention:
>
> *O*rganic olive oil bought should state on the label, the title BIO.

These olive oil producers provide an oil which is rich in organic characteristics. Olive oil extraction is done under strict conditions of processing, where no chemicals are permitted nor heat in the press and no other techniques are used which might affect its characteristics.

In countries of the European Union (including Greece, of course), organic products are strongly protected by law and are carefully checked by quality control organizations. Organic oil is usually extra virgin olive oil or just virgin.

PRACTICAL ADVICE

✻ Good olive oil has a pleasant taste and smell. In general, Virgin olive oil extra should always be chosen. If the level of acidity is mentioned, make sure it is of a low level. International agreement states that virgin olive oil extra should have an acidity level between 0.1 and 1. Recently, some bottles have included exact information regarding this matter (i.e. 0.4 or 0.5). This is a good sign which gives the consumer the choice of a high quality oil or a poor, blended olive oil.

BLENDING

✻ In general, olive oil is technically quite easy to mix with seed oil. This might be done by disreputable traders who sell unbottled olive oil but it is impossible for established oil producers to do something like this when they have their name on the product. It is difficult for a consumer to realize unless he has a great experience in tasting olive oil. Technology now can detect the slightest forgery. So no reputable oil producer would ever endanger his reputation...

> **ADVICE:**
>
> Olive oil resembles set fat when below zero degrees Celsius. Seed oils remain liquid at these temperatures. If unsure about the quality of your oil, do your own experiment to see if it is a forgery.

A. VIRGIN OLIVE OIL

✻ In general, virgin olive oil is, regardless of its quality level, a natural product, which has not had its characteristics altered, has been extracted naturally, without chemicals or other processing and the heat during pressing which does not exceed 33° Celsius cannot affect its quality. It is the oil used in most olive oil producing areas in Greece and the same referred to by medical studies, which proved that the Cretan diet is the healthiest in the Mediterranean. This oil retains all its natural characteristics which have been pressed out of the olive fruit, including various trace elements and vitamins.

1. Virgin olive oil extra

Exceptional quality olive oil. Particular natural flavour and taste. Acidity ranges between 0.1-1 (0.1 –1 grams oleic acid per 100 grams olive oil).

2. Virgin olive oil – fine

Olive oil with excellent smell and taste. Acidity can reach 1.5 grams oleic acid per 100 grams olive oil.

3. Virgin olive oil semi-fine

A virgin olive oil with a good taste and smell. Acidity can reach 3.3 grams oleic acid per 100 grams olive oil.

4. Virgin olive oil lampante

Taste and smell are not good. It cannot be consumed without being refined. Acidity can reach 3.3%.

B. REFINED OLIVE OIL

�֍ This comes from the industrial type of oil "lampante". It has a bad smell and taste so it needs to be processed in order to be made edible. The refining eliminates the bad smell and taste so that the oil attains neutral characteristics. The main problem with refined oil is the down-grade of its characteristics and a decrease in its vitamin value as well as other important agents it contains, such as tocopherols and sterols. Refined oil tends to be the same bright colour which extra virgin olive oil has. It is light yellow colour without smell or taste which would attract interest, in other words, neutral. The production of refined oil is limited in Greece in comparison with other oil producing countries which use this method on the larger part of their production. Greek olive oil is a high quality product and does not need to be processed in order to be consumed. That is why the inhabitants of areas where high quality olive oil is consumed, find it difficult to accept anything less.

C. PURE OLIVE OIL

✖ It is a product which answers the market's demands. It is basically a refined olive oil, to which virgin oil is added to improve its character. Unfortunately there are no set levels of blending refined olive oil with virgin olive oil. Thus, there could be 50% virgin oil in a mixture or just 10%! The neutral refined oil can easily attain an improved colour, taste and smell. Industries that deal with its promotion have come up with their own levels in a mixture so as to improve the quality but at the same time, keep the price down. The Greek consumer who is used to the taste of good virgin olive oil has difficulty in using it...
Acidity level may reach 1.5%.

D. OLIVE RESIDUE OIL

✖ Chemical methods (solvents) are used to dissolve oil from the residue. Olive stones are woody and the oil which remains cannot be removed

naturally, so it is removed through distillation with the use of solvents. Acidity does not exceed 1.5%.

EXTRA VIRGIN OLIVE OIL
UP TO 90%!

✖ Greek olive oil producers offer extra virgin olive oil at a percentage of 80-85%. In some areas, such as Crete, this figure is greater, as much as 85-90% and tends to increase!

CHEMICAL COMPOSITION OF OLIVE OIL

✖ Olive oil is a fluid fatty product containing important constituents which give it unique characteristics. Among these are:

Organic acids
Vitamins
Colouring substances
Hydrocarbons
Minerals (micronutrients etc.)

ADVICE:

Extra virgin olive oil may be a little more expensive but the quality is much better. It is a totally natural product which should be used instead of butter in cooking and on salads. It really is a matter of health!

The fatty acids of olive oil are classified into saturated acids (palmitic, stearic etc) and unsaturated acids (oleic, linoleic, linolenic). The unsaturated acids are again classified into monounsaturated and polyunsaturated acids. In general, the unsaturated acids are liquid whereas the saturated are solid. At normal temperatures, olive oil remains liquid and this is due to its large amount of unsaturated compounds.

The fatty acids contained in olive oil are:

Omega 9 oleic 63-83%
Palmitic 7.0-17%
Palmitoleic 0.3-3.0%
Omega 6 Linoleic 3.5-14%
Stearic 0.5-5.0%
Omega 3 Linolenic 0.01-1.5%
Myristic 0.0-0.1%
Arachidic 0.0-0.8%

Olive oils from the more southerly regions of the Mediterranean tend to be higher in linoleic acid than in the northerly regions.

OTHER SUBSTANCES

Tocopherols 150-170mg/kg
An excellent source of vitamin E. They protect against LDL oxidation (peroxidation, a dominant risk factor for the development of atheromatosis).
Phenols, polyphenols, phenolic acids
They have an important antioxidative effect and protect olive oil from high temperatures.
Sterols and especially **β sitosterol**
This can only be found in olive oil. Its effect is extremely important as it counters intestinal absorption of dietary cholesterol.
Hydrocarbons (squalene, β-carotene etc.)
These also have an antioxidative effect. Recent studies have shown that substances like squalene can even lessen the rate of growth of breast cancer and may be other cancers.
Alcohols (terpenic alcohols)
It is believed to help the distancing of cholesterol through the increase of bile production.
The **colouring substances** in olive oil
β-carotene
a-chlorophyll
β-chlorophyll
These substances are extremely useful in metabolism, cell renewal and wound healing.

DIGESTION OF OLIVE OIL

※ Olive oil is easily digested. The human body absorbs the vitamins contained in this natural product. Research has proved that only breast milk can be digested more easily by the human body! The make up of fat in breast milk is similar to that in olive oil.

WHY OLIVE OIL ONLY?

※ Olive oil should be used instead of any other fat on the market. It is the only one produced in a natural way and it keeps its characteristics intact. Seed oil is the result of chemical processes! In other words, there is no room for comparison.

Various myths have been circulated that seed oil is lighter or better than olive oil but this has proved completely false in scientific research.

Olive oil is not heavier than any other oil, as all the fat agents have nearly all the same calories! In addition, olive oil is rich in antioxidative agents (those which have an anti-cancer effect) while medical studies point out the health value to people.

WHICH OLIVE OIL?

※ Without doubt, the best olive oil is the extra virgin one. It is actually olive juice. It can be used for cooking, in place of animal fats and other fatty substances. It can be used on bread in place of butter or on salads. A little bread (usually a dried rusk) soaked with olive oil has always been a good solution for a Greek's breakfast or a snack. On Crete, the island where the inhabitants, according to the World Health Organization and other medical studies in the last forty years, have the best health, dipping bread in olive oil is common practice. Villagers can be seen to eat salads with fresh vegetables "swimming" in olive oil and at the end, bread is used to wipe up the last of the olive oil! Extra virgin olive oil is a little more expensive than virgin oil, more expensive than "pure olive oil" (a blend of virgin and refined olive oil) and definitely more expensive than refined oil. But the difference in the price is not so great to be unaffordable.

GREEN COLOURED OLIVE OIL

※ This will probably have been made from green olives which have been collected before having ripened and sometimes, as has already been mentioned, the colour is a result of other factors, too. Usually, green-coloured olive oil has a pepper-like taste. It can be used for cooking pulses and vegetables, game or meat, although it is a matter of personal choice.

GOLDEN-YELLOW OLIVE OIL

This probably comes from olives that had started to turn reddish or black. It generally has a milder taste, more fruity and gives off a

GENERALLY

Extra virgin olive oil is not expensive. As a valuable ally in health, it is worth much more than the price paid.

variety of aromas. The smell may be reminiscent of fruit or vanilla. This is the oil usually chosen by chefs especially when cooking fish. But all these points are matters of personal choice. Good extra virgin olive oil can be used for many purposes, even for sweets or cakes. In traditional Greek cooking, only olive oil is used for this baking and the oil is generally of a very high standard.

HOW TO JUDGE EXTRA VIRGIN OLIVE OIL?

A wise consumer should read the label on olive oil containers. These give details that will help to make the right choice. The colour may range from green to golden-yellow but this is never a sure sign of quality. So, always read the label on the outside,

EXTRA VIRGIN OLIVE OIL
then look at various other points:

1. Date of bottling and expiry date. In other words, the period of time an oil producer can guarantee his product. Olive oil can last for up to a year and a half in a good container, even a little longer.

2. Level of acidity. The degree of acidity is now printed on the outside label. The consumer can then ascertain what he wants to buy. Olive oil with an acidity level less than 5 is considered excellent.

3. Area of production. Region and country of origin. There are many areas well known for olive oil. Shouldn't we know them?

4. The amount in the container. Work out the price per litre.

5. Especially for organic olive oil, take care that there is the exact indication on the label that has been established for organic products. Look for a guarantee from an organization.

6. The trade name is not enough. Know the name of the oil producer or company. A responsible producer always ensures that there is information about the product so that it reaches you in the best condition.

The extra virgin olive oil has its own distinct smell, taste and so cannot be neutral. Olive oil with no taste and of a light colour is usually a product of refining.

OLIVE OIL, THE SECRET OF HEALTH

※ It is known world-wide that olive oil acts as a shield of protection regarding our health, when taking into account cardiovascular diseases, cancer, even diabetes and other diseases. More and more research is being done which shows the great value of olive oil as a perfect food for man.

BAD CHOLESTEROL: The consumption of olive oil instead of other fats or oils reduces the concentration of LDL cholesterol in the blood without decreasing the levels of HDL, the so-called "bad" and "good" cholesterol respectively!

TRIGLYCERIDES: It has been shown that olive oil reduces the level of triglycerides in the blood.
A collection of bad cholesterol and triglycerides in the blood can block the arteries which transport oxygen to the brain and heart.
In general, olive oil protects against heart diseases.

HYPERTENSION: Olive oil reduces blood pressure, both systolic and diastolic. Therefore it decreases the risk of heart attacks and strokes.

CANCER: Recent studies have shown that olive oil consumption can slow down breast cancer and other types of cancer. A balanced diet with olive oil and vegetables can reduce the chances of the appearance of cancer by 75%.

GASTROINTESTINAL SYSTEM: Recent research shows that olive oil in conjunction with a healthy diet (vegetables, little meat etc)
*protects against cancer of the stomach
*makes the liver work better
*helps the liver to detoxify poisonous substances

OSTEOPOROSIS: Olive oil assists in the maintenance of bone thickness and protects against osteoporosis.

RHEUMATOID ARTHRITIS: Olive oil consumption reduces the chances of the appearance of this condition by 75%, especially with a balanced diet and the consumption of more fish.

DIABETES: Olive oil should also be included in the treatment of diabetes.

OLIVE OIL IN COOKING.
SCENTED OILS

The techniques which were used in ancient times in scenting oils were simple. Aromatic plants were left in oil until the desired scent was achieved or otherwise different methods with heating were used. The ability of olive oil to change its smell was well-known in the days of Aristotle (384-322 B.C.).

The philosopher Theophrastus (around 372-288 B.C.) recorded much information about the process of scenting olive oil to make perfumes. He refers to many scented oils, besides rose-scented oil, in which they added parts of other plants, such as lentisk, gorse, sweet flag. Apple olive oil was flavoured with apple which was left in the oil until it started to turn black and then was replaced with another. At the end of symposiums in ancient times, aromatic oil was offered to the guests. In Roman times, scented oil was used only in caring for the body. Today it is mainly used for cooking purposes.

Olive oil scented with dill in Byzantium
🐾 In Byzantine times, it was not unusual for oil to be scented with herbs and aromatic plants. It was customary for aromatic plants to be placed into olive oil jars, if only to improve on the characteristics of a certain oil.

Liburnic olive oil, scented with laurel leaves
🐾 This was a well-known oil in Roman times but Palladius (4th century A.D.) states that it was of Greek descent. The making of this oil is known due to the writings of Apicius and also from "Geoponica", of the period of Porphyrogennetus.

Scented oils in later periods
🐾 Ancient traditions could not be forgotten easily. There is no full picture as to how this practice continued through the centuries or if it was forgotten totally in some areas but it seems to have survived in some areas of Crete…

In the area of Kastelli, Pediada, on Crete, up until the first few decades of the 20th century at least, they used to put a bunch of oregano in the jar with the oil which was to be used for cooking.

HOW TO MAKE
SCENTED OLIVE OIL

Scented olive oil can be made using aromatic plants, fresh or dried, spices, garlic, hot pepper, or the peel of citrus fruits. These could be used on their own or in combination with others.

The olive oil to be used has to be of good quality and of low acidity. In order to accept the scents of the herbs or the other ingredients, the oil should not have its own strong smell. Some use refined olive oil or pure olive oil because it is neutral in taste. In this way though, the advantages of extra virgin olive oil are lost. Extra virgin olive oil with a mild taste can be used. The results are wonderful as a totally natural product is consumed with all its benefits.

Bottles used for storage should be clean and dry. The aromatic plants used should also be clean and dry.

The bottles with olive oil should not be left in the sun but kept in dark, cool places.

Scented oil can serve as a lovely starter when on small dried rusks or bread. It is the best substitute for butter and it has no cholesterol. It can also be added to salads, boiled vegetables, roasted meat or fish, rice, potatoes, pastry and also used as a basic ingredient of sauces. Slices of bread drizzled with scented olive oil, such as with rosemary, garlic or hot pepper, can be browned in the oven or under the grill.

Naturally, olive oil has an array of smells, but by experimenting with aromatic plants in different combinations, a choice of scent can be made. It is not a bad idea to have a few bottles of scented olive oil to be used for different purposes.

If you want to quickly scent olive oil, heat the aromatic plants in a small amount of olive oil, then filter through a clean cloth and add to the main body of oil.

Olive oil with aromatic plants

🌰 Olive oil can be scented with all types of aromatic plants: rosemary, fennel, dill, mint, basil, parsley etc. A bottle of olive oil can be scented with a sprig of each of these plants or two or three together.

If using only one plant, place 2-3 sprigs, washed and dried, in a bottle with 2 cups of olive oil. Store the bottle in a cool, dark place for about ten days before using it. The plants can be left in the bottle to add to the scent visually, but not for too long as they can spoil the oil. Thus it is better to remove the plants once the olive oil is scented.

Olive oil scented with mint, parsley and fennel or dill is very successful.

Olive oil scented with basil

🌰 In a bottle, put 3-4 sprigs of basil which has been washed and dried, along with 2 cloves of garlic, which is optional. Add 2 cups of extra virgin olive oil and cap the bottle tightly. The scented oil will be ready in about 10 days.

Olive oil with basil goes perfectly with uncooked vegetables but especially tomatoes. (Imagine slices of tomatoes topped with feta cheese or sour mizithra and drizzled over with basil scented oil). It also goes well in tomato sauces and is superb for dunking pieces of bread.

Olive oil scented with fennel

🌰 In a bottle, put 2 cloves of garlic, which is optional, 2-3 cloves and 3-4 sprigs of fennel which has been washed and dried. Depending on the season, fennel seeds can be used and 1 tablespoon is enough. Add a litre of olive oil and leave for 2 weeks before using.

Olive oil scented with oregano

🌰 It is better to use fresh oregano for its strong smell.

In a bottle with 2 cups olive oil, place 2-3 sprigs of fresh oregano or 2 tablespoons of dried herb, cap the bottle tightly and store in a dark, cool place. It can be used after 10 days and can be added to anything, from salads to meat and fish. The smell of this oil is similar to the one with basil. It can also be complemented with lemon.

Olive oil scented with herbs

🌿 In a large bottle olive oil, about 4 cups, you can place many herbs together such as 2-3 sprigs of oregano, 1 teaspoon thyme, 1 teaspoon dried mint and 1 teaspoon dried basil. The result, after several days, is a superbly scented oil which can be used for many dishes. The oil can be filtered through a cloth or coffee filter to remove the herbs.

Don't forget to use scented olive oil at the beginning of a meal on bread or dried rusk instead of butter. This olive oil with herbs is among the most suitable to be used.

Olive oil with garlic

🌿 Mash 4 cloves of garlic and mix with 4 tablespoons olive oil in a blender. Filter this through a cloth or a coffee filter and transfer to a bottle with 2 more cups of olive oil. It should be kept in a cool, dark place.

Olive oil scented with garlic goes perfectly with grilled slices of bread, spaghetti, soups, sauces, roasted meat and fish, salads and uncooked vegetables.

Olive oil with garlic and rosemary

🌿 In a bottle with 2 cups of olive oil, put 2 cloves of garlic, 1 sprig of fresh rosemary and 5-6 peppercorns. Cap the bottle tightly and keep in a dark, cool place. When you start to use the oil, after about 10 days, remove garlic and rosemary.

The scent of rosemary can go with other smells. It is wonderful with roast potatoes, aubergines, lamb or marinated fried fish.

Olive oil scented with citrus fruits

🌿 In a bottle with 2 cups of olive oil, put the peel from half lemon and half an orange and cap tightly. The oil is ready in 10 days. Remove the peel after 2 months to keep the oil longer. Store in a dark, cool place.

Olive oil scented with citrus fruits is wonderful on salads, boiled greens, fish or meat, or to scent cakes or sweets such as pies or biscuits.

Citrus fruits can be combined with other aromatic plants, for example lemon with fennel, or with herbs.

Oil scented with oregano and lemon peel or thyme and lemon peel is a great success.

Olive oil with lemon

🌸 Clean and dry three small lemons. Place 3 cloves in each lemon.

Put these in a jar and add 1 litre of olive oil. Keep in a dark, cool place.

Olive oil with hot pepper

🌸 In a bottle with 2 cups of olive oil add 2-3 dry hot peppers or fresh ones to scent the oil which can be used with many dishes. This can be enhanced by adding various spices to produce the oil to your taste.

Use after about 2 weeks and keep in a cool place away from the rays of the sun.

It can be used to accompany greens, especially that which is grilled, as well as omelets, tomato sauces used in pastries, meat and all kinds of pulses.

Olive oil with hot pepper and laurel leaves

🌿 To the previous oil, 3-4 laurel leaves can be added, having been washed and dried.

Olive oil with spices

🌿 2 cups of olive oil can be scented with 5-6 peppercorns, 4-5 pimento pods, 1 teaspoon cumin and a stick of cinnamon. This scented oil is suitable for spicy dishes.

Olive oil with cinnamon and clove

🌿 In a bottle with 2 cups of oil, put 2-3 sticks of cinnamon and 5-6 cloves. Store the bottle and use the oil after a few days, especially in sweet dishes.

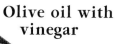

Olive oil with vinegar

🌿 This can be made with the same ingredients and combinations used in making scented oil. The ratio of oil to vinegar depends on personal taste. Normally a ratio of 4:1 is used.

OLIVE OIL
IN THE PRESERVATION OF FOOD

Products in traditional Greek cooking were made in abundance in the summer months and then preserved in various ways for the winter-time. Preservation of food is a way of life, especially in the past few decades, when it contributed to household expenses. Suitable techniques were used to ensure housewives did not throw away surplus products. It is impressive that the preservation of food in Greek dietary tradition kept the original flavours even after several months. Fresh vegetables could be dried in the sun, as were fruit, so that they

could be stored for a long time, providing a rich source of calories on cold, winter days.

"The method of preservation is simple", emphasized a study by the Rockefeller Foundation on Crete (1948) and it explained *"products are either dried in the sun or in the oven"*...

Olive oil plays a leading role in the preservation of food, the tasty products which are kept in jars or bottles. Together with vinegar and salt, it has been used to preserve food since ancient times. It is a natural product for preservation as it blocks air from coming into contact with the food. That is why food is placed in oil or it is covered with a thick layer of oil for protection.

Although today we can find all fruits nearly all year round, jars with pickled products in the kitchen are always thought well and offer variety at the table. The season for each fruit or vegetable can be exploited as it is then at its cheapest.

Many kinds of food can be kept in olive oil: meat, fish, vegetables, cheese. Products to be preserved should be completely dry, as water favours the growth of microorganisms. Also, the jars must be clean and dry. Boil them in water and then leave to dry on a clean towel or in the oven for a while. Fill jars when cool. Close with a lid which has been cleaned as above.

To preserve vegetables, they must be fresh and of good quality. Usually they are boiled for a few minutes in vinegar and then covered in olive oil. The vinegar should not be of a dark colour in order not to colour the vegetables. Salt should not be left out so that they do not soften.

The jar should not be filled to the brim but a small space should be left at the top. Don't forget to put a label on the jar with the date of making and contents.

If you keep the jars in the fridge the oil will thicken but it returns to normal if it is left at room temperature for a while.

Pickled bulbs

🌿 Bulbs of the plant Muscari comosum are indigenous to the Mediterranean countries. They can be found in many European shops but are difficult to get hold of in America. Usually a starter but folklore medicine uses them as a diuretic, a tonic and an aphrodisiac. Bulbs are now cultivated in many Mediterranean countries.

1	kg bulbs
2-3	teaspoons salt
3	cloves garlic in thin slices
	or 2-3 fresh garlic leaves, roughly cut
½	cup roughly chopped dill
5-6	peppercorns
2	cups white vinegar
1	cup olive oil

Clean the bulbs like the onions and wash them. Boil them for half an hour, changing the water 2-3 times. The last time, add salt. Once cooked, remove from heat and dry on kitchen roll.

Simmer vinegar, garlic, peppercorns and dill and leave to cool. Strain the vinegar and pour over the bulbs which have been put in a jar. Pour in the olive oil and keep in the fridge for quite a while. They can be eaten after 1-2 days, garnished with a little finely chopped dill.

Pickled peppers in olive oil

1   kg peppers (preferably red ones)
1   tbsp black peppercorns
1   teaspoon salt
1   cup olive oil
1   cup vinegar
2-3 laurel leaves
2-3 cloves garlic

Wash peppers, remove seeds and grill for about 20 minutes until the skin blisters. Allow to cool and then peel.

In a pan, slowly boil for five minutes the vinegar, peppercorns, garlic, salt and laurel leaves. Strain the vinegar and leave to cool.

Put the peppers in a jar and pour on the vinegar. Add the olive oil to cover the peppers. Close the jar and keep in the fridge for 20 days or more.

Pickled aubergines in olive oil

1   kg long aubergines
2   cups vinegar
3   teaspoons salt
2   mashed hot peppers
     or 1 tablespoon peppercorns
1   small bunch roughly cut celery
3-4 cloves finely chopped garlic
2-3 tbsps dried oregano
2-3 cups olive oil

🐾 Clean and wash aubergines. Cut into thin slices and boil for five minutes in a pan with 2 cups vinegar, 6 cups water and 3 teaspoons salt. Drain immediately and leave to cool.
In a jar, place a layer of aubergines, scatter on celery, garlic, oregano, pepper, drizzle a little olive oil and continue this procedure until all the ingredients have been used. At the end, pour in the olive oil to totally cover and close the jar or jars if one is not enough. They keep for 2-3 months in a cool, dry place and can be eaten after 3-4 days.
Alternatively, whole small aubergines can be used which can be pickled in the same way.

Lemons in olive oil

4-5 thick-skinned lemons
1   tbsp salt
1   tbsps dried oregano
2   cups olive oil

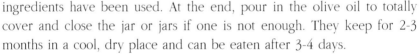

🐾 Put the lemons in a bowl of water and leave them there for two days to rid of their bitterness.
Dry on kitchen roll, cut into horizontal slices, season with salt and place in a jar, sprinkling a little oregano after each layer.
Cover the lemons in olive oil, close the jar and keep in cool, dry place. These garnish meat and fish, especially when grilled.

Beetroot in olive oil and vinegar

1   kg beetroot
4-5 cloves garlic
2   cups vinegar
½   cup olive oil
3   teaspoons salt

🌢 Wash beetroot well and boil in water with salt until soft. Dry, peel and cut into slices. Put in a jar with chopped garlic imbetween. Pour in the vinegar and cover with olive oil. Keep in a cool place and wait 2-3 days before using.

Octopus in olive oil and vinegar

1   kg octopus
2-3 bay leaves
5-6 peppercorns
½   cup vinegar
½   cup olive oil

🌢 Wash the octopus or octopuses and place in a pan with the bay leaves and peppercorns. Cook on a low heat in its own juices until tender. If needed, add vinegar. Once the octopus has cooled, cut into small pieces and place in a jar. Add vinegar and then olive oil. Oil that has been scented with garlic is preferred. Close the jar and store in a cool place.

Pilchard or sardines in vinegar and olive oil

🌢 Clean the fish removing heads and guts. Place in a bowl with salt and vinegar to cover. (If the vinegar is too strong, dilute with a little water). Leave pilchard in vinegar for about 10 hours and sardines for 24 to 30 hours depending upon their size. Test by pulling the tail and if it moves and the insides are rather white than red, then they are ready. The fish can be filleted or left as they are.
Place the fish in a medium bowl and cover with olive oil. You can garnish with parsley and thin slices of garlic. They can be kept in the fridge quite a while.

SAUCES AND DIPS WITH OLIVE OIL

O live oil is the basic ingredient in sauces, along with lemon juice, vinegar or eggs. This is also true for dips, those sauces which are thick and almost set and are used as appetizers before a meal, with the first drink.

Dips are usually used with small items such as vegetables, but also cheese and even bread or dried rusks to be dipped into the set sauce. They can even accompany main courses. These not only offer interesting varieties of taste but also encourage a healthy style of eating due to the olive oil used. Although they may seem like a recent gastronomic variety, many of these dips are well known and loved all over Greece. Tzatziki, taramosalata, aubergine salad and many others have, for centuries, had a place in Greek cuisine. In this case we must look to see if there is a grain of truth in the housewife's philosophy, the person who was responsible for the diet of the family in the past. The strict fasting in the Greek Orthodox Lent encouraged cooking to reach new heights as it was forced to use the fruits of the land and the ingenuity of the Greek housewife. A taramosalata, for instance, made a meal during Lent much tastier, more varied and it could be stored for days. The same can be said for tomato sauce. Humus (chickpea purée) has a special taste and can be seen not only in Greek cookery (especially the islands) but also in various Arab countries.

Meat could be accompanied by tzatziki or tyrokafteri. The mashed pulses were sometimes the main dishes and at others, the starter. As always, the leading ingredient in all these recipes was olive oil! This could transform a traditional dish into something of great demand, especially in the areas where it was abundant and of good quality. Along with the traditional recipes we can now also add others which have been altered from their original form. Set sauces or dips can be used not only at home but also in places where people gather. These have been used to great effect!

Oil and lemon dressing

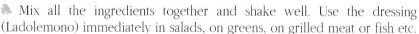

1   cup olive oil
½   cup lemon juice
1   teaspoon salt
     pepper, oregano,
     thyme or parsley (optional)

🐾 Mix all the ingredients together and shake well. Use the dressing (Ladolemono) immediately in salads, on greens, on grilled meat or fish etc.

Oil and vinegar dressing

Made in exactly the same way and with the same ingredients as the oil and lemon dressing, only replacing the lemon juice with good vinegar made from wine (lathoxido). It goes well with fried foods especially fish, meat some salads and greens.

Egg-lemon sauce (Avgolemono)

It gives flavour and thickens soups and sauces in various dishes

2   eggs, juice of 2 lemons
2   cups liquid from the food for which avgolemono
    is prepared

Beat first the whites and then the yolks of the eggs, until frothy, 2-3 minutes. Add lemon juice, beating constantly and then a few ladles of the liquid from the food in the pot until the egg and lemon mixture is warm. Remove pot from heat, pour in egg mixture and shake the pot to mix the egg-lemon mixture with the food.

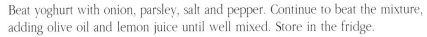

Yoghurt dip with parsley

300 grams strained yoghurt
2   tablespoons dried parsley
1   small grated onion
      salt and pepper
2   tablespoons olive oil
1   tablespoon lemon juice

Beat yoghurt with onion, parsley, salt and pepper. Continue to beat the mixture, adding olive oil and lemon juice until well mixed. Store in the fridge.

Parsley dip

1   large bunch parsley (only the leaves)
1   slice stale bread (2 cm thick)
1   small onion
1   clove garlic
     juice of 1 lemon
2   tablespoons olive oil
300 grams strained yoghurt
½   teaspoon salt, pepper

Soak the bread in water, strain and place in a blender with parsley, onion, garlic, salt and pepper. Blend the mixture and then add yoghurt, olive oil and lemon juice which we mix in. Parsley salad is used either as an accompaniment to fresh vegetables, boiled eggs or fish or alone as a salad, garnished with parsley leaves and olives.

Yoghurt dip with mint

300 grams strained yoghurt
1 tablespoon dried mint
  salt, pepper
1 tablespoon lemon juice

In a deep bowl, beat yoghurt with mint, salt and pepper. Then add olive oil and lemon juice. Beat until well mixed. Keep in the fridge. This goes well mainly with fresh fish.

Yoghurt dip with dill

300 grams strained yoghurt
1 tablespoon dried dill
1 mashed clove garlic
  salt, pepper
2 tablespoons olive oil
1 tablespoon lemon juice

In a deep bowl, beat yoghurt with dill, garlic, salt and pepper. Add olive oil and lemon juice. Beat until well mixed. Keep in the fridge.
This goes well with vegetables and green salads.

Avocado dip

2 avocados
½ teaspoon salt
½ teaspoon pepper
1 small grated onion
2 tbsps finely chopped parsley
2 tbsps lemon juice
2 tbsps olive oil

Peel avocado, remove the stone and then mash it in a deep bowl. Add the other ingredients and beat with a whisk until creamy.
Garnish with parsley and keep the dip in the fridge. Use it on its own to dip appetizers and small vegetable pieces or on meat or fish or even on salads.

Garlic and potato dip with walnuts or almonds (skordalia)

1   kg potatoes
6-8 cloves finely chopped garlic
½   teaspoon salt
½   cup olive oil
4   tbsps lemon juice or vinegar
150 grams roughly ground walnuts or almonds

Boil potatoes and before they go entirely cold, peel and put them in a blender along with garlic, salt, olive oil and lemon juice or vinegar. At the end, add walnuts or almonds until the mixture becomes creamy. If skordalia is too thick a little stock from the fish that it usually accompanies can be added.
This puree also goes well with fried vegetables.

Aubergine dip

½   kg aubergines
2   mashed cloves garlic
    or 1 grated medium onion
    salt, pepper
2   tbsps finely chopped parsley
1   teaspoon dried oregano
3   tbsps lemon juice
1   tbsp vinegar
4-5 tbsps olive oil
2   tbsps roughly ground almonds

Wash aubergines and cook in their skins either under the grill or on the cooking ring, having been wrapped in aluminum foil, until they soften. Remove from heat, cool slightly and then peel and remove as many seeds as possible.
Place aubergines in a deep bowl and combine with remaining ingredients until smooth.
Garnish with olives and caper.

Almond dip with yoghurt

1   kg strained yoghurt
½   teaspoon salt
½   cup finely chopped dill
½   cup whitened, roasted, finely
    chopped almonds
½   cup olive oil
2   tbsps lemon juice

With a fork or a whisk, beat yoghurt with salt, olive oil and lemon juice. Then add dill and almonds. Combine well.

Garlic, cucumber and yoghurt dip (Tzatziki)

½   kg strained yoghurt
2   large cucumbers
3   cloves garlic
½   teaspoon salt
4-5 tbsps olive oil
2   tbsps vinegar
1   tbsp finely chopped mint or dill (optional)

Peel and grate cucumbers. Squeeze as hard as possible to remove water completely. Mash garlic with salt in a mortar. In a medium-size bowl, mix yoghurt with cucumber and garlic. Slowly add vinegar and olive oil and combine well. Finally add mint or parsley. Refrigerate until ready to use.

Cod Roe Dip (Taramosalata)

In the fasting periods of the Orthodox church which last for long, some particular dishes are usually made, one of which is taramosalata. It is a traditional food on Clean Monday and the first days of the Holy Week before Easter Sunday. Apart from its use as a food for fasting, it is a well-known Greek appetizer. It is made from cod roe. Cod roe is the preserved eggs from various types of fish such as carp, grey mullet etc. It is sold either packed or loose. There are two types, the pink and the light pink, which Greeks describe as white. The light pink is more expensive but is the best because it does not contain colouring agents.

100 grams taramas (cod roe), preferably white
200 grams stale bread
2-3 medium boiled potatoes
½   cup olive oil
4   tbsps lemon juice
1   small grated onion (optional)

Soak bread and squeeze until to get rid of water. Combine cod roe, potatoes, bread and onion in a mixer. Slowly add olive oil and lemon juice alternatively until taramosalata becomes soft and creamy. Garnish with olives and parsley.

Hot cheese dip (Tyrokafteri)

½   kg crumbled feta cheese*
2   hot green peppers
6   tbsps olive oil
    juice of 2 lemons
1   tbsp oregano or finely chopped dill (optional)

First cook peppers in a frying pan with 2 tbsps olive oil or in the oven and blend them in the mixer. While running, add feta cheese, oregano or dill, remaining olive oil and lastly lemon juice until tyrokafteri becomes soft and creamy.

* The Greek feta cheese is a unique product exclusively made from sheep's or goat's milk. These animals live freely in the Greek mountains. Feta cheese produced outside Greece is made with cow's milk. The cheese is kept in salty water, cut into blocks, fetes in Greek wherefrom its name comes. The fresh milk is heated on low heat and rennin is added (an enzyme taken from the mucous membrane of the stomach of young animals). When the cheese sets it is put in wooden containers in order to be strained. Then it is cut into blocks (fetes), salted and packed.

Chickpea purée - Hummus

A purée of chick peas is well known in many Greek areas as a superb starter. It was even made in ancient Greece and since then, the practice of mashing pulses has become common place in order to make a wide range of main courses and starters.

200	grams chick peas
2	cloves garlic
½ - 1	teaspoon salt
1/3	teaspoon pepper
1/3	teaspoon cumin
3	tbsps olive oil
3	tbsps tahin (ground sesame seeds)
3	tbsps water
4	tbsps lemon juice
1	teaspoon paprika (red pepper)
	parsley

Soak chick peas the night before in a large bowl with water. The next day, boil them until soft. Drain and allow to cool. In a bowl, dilute tahin with water. Put chick peas into a mixer and, grinding constantly, add salt, tahin, garlic, pepper, olive oil and lemon juice until hummus becomes smooth and creamy. Serve cold, sprinkled with paprika and garnished with finely chopped parsley.

Yoghurt and carrot dip

½	kg carrots
300	grams strained yoghurt
2	cloves mashed garlic
1	teaspoon salt
3-4	tbsps olive oil
1	tbsp lemon juice
½	cup roughly ground walnuts (optional)

Scrape the carrots and grate them (or grind) in the mixer.
Whip yoghurt with remaining ingredients, throw in the carrot and mix well.

Dressing with garlic and walnuts

1	cup slightly roasted walnuts
2	cloves garlic
1	medium onion (optional)
2	tbsps finely chopped parsley or basil
7-8	tbsps olive oil

Put all the ingredients into a blender and combine well. This dressing goes perfectly with spaghetti and other pastas.

Yoghurt and courgette dip

½   kg courgettes
300 grams strained yoghurt
2   mashed garlic cloves
2   tbsps finely chopped dill or mint
3-4 tbsps olive oil
1   tbsp lemon juice
      salt, pepper
5-6 black olives

Wash and cut courgettes in pieces. Boil in salted water until tender and drain well. (It is easier to drain them if placed in a cloth and squeezed). Put them in a salad bowl and mash completely with a fork. Add yoghurt, garlic, dill, olive oil, lemon juice salt and pepper and combine well. Garnish with olives.

OLIVES IN TRADITIONAL COOKING

In Mediterranean cooking, the olive is used to its best in cooking, being the prime ingredient of various delicious starters and renowned for its individual taste. This custom is best seen in the farming communities where it is more readily available. It is mainly consumed in its natural form and can be used to accompany a variety of dishes. Without cooking, the olive is hardly missing from the Greeks' diet and this has made the farming population accustomed to its taste and so they have tried to find different ways of using it in cooking.

Meat stew with olives

1	kg meat (veal, pork, chicken or rabbit)
½	cup olive oil
2	small onions, finely chopped
	or 3-4 fresh onions
3-4	medium- sized tomatoes, peeled,
	seeded and chopped
½	cup white wine
3	tbsps vinegar
1	cinnamon stick
2	laurel leaves
200	grams green olives, cracked or slit
	little salt, pepper

Boil the olives for three minutes in water and then get rid of the water. Do the same process again. Then pit the olives.

Wash meat, scone it and brown in a pan with olive oil and onions. Add wine and vinegar followed by tomatoes, cinnamon, bay leaves and a cup of water. Simmer for half an hour and then add the olives. Continue cooking for about 15 minutes, adding, if needed, a little water.

In the same way, we can cook fish (grouper, cod, sea bream) with olives.

Octopus with olives

1	octopus (1.5 kilos)
½	cup olive oil
1	small onion, finely chopped
½	cup red wine
1	clove finely chopped garlic
1	teaspoon peppercorns
2-3	bay leaves
150	grams green olives

Boil the olives for three minutes in water and pour it out. Do the same process again, then pit the olives.

Wash the octopus and remove eyes, mouth, stomach and ink.

Place in a pan and gently cook until all its own juices have evaporated. Then add olive oil and onion until brown. Wine should then be introduced. Add garlic, bay leaves and pepper. Cook for 5-6 minutes and then add olives and a little water. Cook a while longer until it is completely done.

Cuttlefish with olives and spinach

1	kg cuttlefish
1	kg spinach
½	cup olive oil
2	medium-sized dried onions or 5-6 fresh onions
½	cup white wine
1	bunch fennel or dill, finely chopped
½	bunch mint, finely chopped
	a little salt, pepper
150	grams olives
1	tbsp flour
	juice of 1 lemon

Clean cuttlefish, removing eyes, backbone, stomach and ink. (If desired, keep some of the ink). Re-wash them and cut into pieces. Wash spinach, drain and chop.
Prepare the olives: Boil them in water for about three minutes. Drain them and repeat the process. Then pit the olives. Brown the onion in olive oil and add dill or fennel, mint and cuttlefish. Cook for 10 minutes and then stir in wine and ink (if desired). Simmer for half an hour and then

put in the olives and spinach, very little salt and pepper. Cook for another 10-15 minutes and the dish is ready.

At this point you can thicken the sauce with a diluted solution of one tablespoon of flour with the juice of one lemon. In other words, mix flour with lemon juice, add a little cooking juice from the pan so as to make it dissolve quicker and then put the mixture into the pan. Stir well and cook for five more minutes.

Tomato sauce with olives

1	medium onion, finely chopped
½	cup olive oil
2	cloves finely chopped garlic
½	kg chopped tomatoes
200	grams pitted olives
	salt, pepper, oregano, basil
½	cup red wine

Prepare the olives: Boil them in water for about three minutes. Drain them and repeat the process. Finally pit them.

Brown the onion in olive oil in a pan and add garlic, tomatoes, wine, olives, salt, if needed, pepper, oregano and basil. Cook on low heat until the sauce thickens. Use it on spaghetti or on grilled fish.

Leeks and celery with olives

½   kg leeks
½   kg celery
½   cup olive oil
1   medium-sized onion, finely chopped
2-3   medium-sized potatoes, cut into quarters
       juice of 1 lemon
200 grams pitted olives

Wash leeks and celery and cut into medium-sized pieces.
Boil the olives changing the water twice to get rid of the salt.
Brown onion in olive oil, add leeks, celery and potatoes along with 1 cup
lukewarm water and simmer for about three quarters
of an hour. Throw in the olives and cook for
10 more minutes. Add lemon juice and the
dish is ready.

Meatballs with green olives

½ kg minced meat
2 cloves finely chopped garlic
1 cup crumbled stale bread
salt, pepper, cumin, to desired taste
1 cup olive oil for frying

For the sauce:

½ cup green olives
3 tbsps olive oil
1 medium finely chopped onion
3 tbsps white wine
½ kg grated tomatoes

Combine minced meat with garlic, bread, ½ teaspoon salt, pepper and cumin and knead well. Shape the meatballs and fry.
Boil the olives 3 times for 3 minutes, changing the water every time. Drain them.
Put 3 tbsps olive oil, the onion and the olives in a pan and brown for 5 minutes. Introduce wine and tomatoes and then cook for 10 minutes. Add meatballs and cook for a further 10 minutes.

Cypriot Olive Bread

1 kg flour (preferably wheat flour)
2 packages dry yeast
½ cup olive oil
1 grated medium-sized onion
1 cup pitted black olives
1 tbsp dried mint
½ teaspoon salt
lentisk seeds, sesame seeds

Dilute yeast in a large bowl with 1 cup warm water and 1 cup flour to make it have a thick porridge-like appearance. Cover with a towel and leave for about half an hour until it bubbles.
Add salt, onion, olive oil, mint, flour and as much water as is needed (about 2 cups).

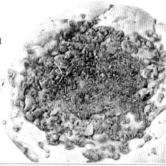

Knead well and when the dough is soft and seemingly elastic, add the olives. Cover the dough and leave it in a warm place to stand for 2 hours until doubled in bulk. Then form a large loaf of bread or many small ones, round or long, and sprinkle with sesame seeds and lentisk seeds. Place immediately in an oiled baking dish and let stand to rise again. When ready place in preheated oven and bake for about 45 minutes.

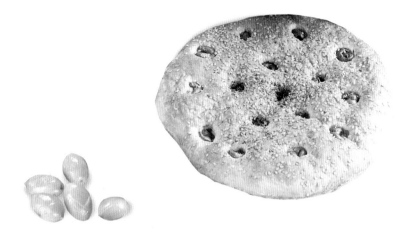

Oven Omelet
with Spinach and Olives

300 grams spinach
3   tbsps olive oil
6   eggs
6   tbsps milk
150 grams grated hard cheese or feta cheese
150 grams pitted olives
100 grams grated toasted bread
    a little salt, pepper

Clean, wash and chop spinach. Then put it in boiling water for 2-3 minutes and drain completely. Heat olive oil in a pan, add spinach and cook for a few minutes until all liquid has evaporated. Whisk egg yolks with milk and add to the spinach along with cheese, olives, bread crumbs, salt, pepper and the egg whites beaten stiff. Mix carefully and pour the mixture into an oven dish. Bake in medium heat for about 20 minutes or until golden brown.

OLIVE OIL IN FRYING

Doctors and dieticians are right with their advice: Fried foods should only be cooked in olive oil! This goes against the myth that animal fats and hydrogenated oils are more resistant to heat, when heated, in comparison to olive oil. Recent studies have shown that olive oil is the most suitable oil for frying because it remains stable due to its anti-oxidization agents, even at high temperatures.

RESISTANT UNTIL UP TO 250° CELSIUS

Animal fats do not have anti-oxidative agents, so as a result, they are oxidized very quickly, with all the harmful effects to the health of those who consume them. Seed oils contain tocopherols (which are anti-oxidative substances) but the great amount of unsaturated acids they contain makes them to get oxidized quickly when they are heated.

Research which has been conducted in the recent years has shown that seed oils spoil at a temperature of 170-180° Celsius. On the other hand olive oil can stand temperatures over 200° C. It is even believed that olive oil can stand temperatures of up to 230-250° Celsius! By olive oil, we mean extra virgin olive oil which is more stable due to its anti-oxidative agents, but even refined olive oil has been proved to resist to heat and remain more stable than seed oil!

The chemical substances also which are contained in hydrogenated oils have been shown to increase "bad" cholesterol and to reduce "good" cholesterol levels in blood.

FEWER CALORIES, MORE VITAMINS

Special research studies carried out in the last few years have refuted one more myth. That is the one which states that fried food absorbs too much oil and so it becomes fattening and bad for the health. If someone tries to use a frying pan correctly, then the crispy crust of food seals in the juices and doesn't let the oil into the food. In order to achieve this crispness, the oil should be allowed to heat, almost to "burn" as they say, yet without being over-heated and producing smoke. Neither should all food be cooked in a frying pan at one time so that the temperature doesn't fall and the frying is done correctly. If the amount of olive oil in the pan diminishes during frying, extra olive oil should be added but only when there is no food in the pan so that the temperature does not drop. It has been proved that foods fried in olive oil absorb less fat in comparison to those fried in seed oils. Therefore, olive oil encourages fewer calories and so it is less fattening! It has also been pointed out that frying doesn't destroy the water-soluble vitamins and the nutritional value of fried food remains almost unaffected.

CAN BE USED MANY TIMES

Olive oil can be used several times for frying, as long as we fry similar things, otherwise the quality of the taste will be affected. But if we fry foods dredged with flour, especially fish, the oil obviously can't be used many times. Yet this oil can be filtered and be used for the frying of similar foods. After 3-5 fries, 30-50% of the vitamins in the olive oil remain unchanged!

Savoury cheese patties

Dough:
- 3 tbsps olive oil
- 2 eggs
- ½ teaspoon salt
- ½ kg all purpose flour
- ½ cup water

Filling:
- ½ kg grated kefalotyri cheese*
- 4 eggs

Combine the ingredients for the dough and make a firm mixture. Cover and refrigerate for half an hour. Whisk the eggs and mix in the cheese. Roll out the dough and cut circles the size of a saucer. Put 1-2 teaspoons of filling on each circle. Fold in two to make a semi-circle and press down the edges so that they stick. This can be done with a fork's prongs.
Fry the patties in very hot olive oil and serve sprinkled with grated cheese.

*Kefalotyri: A hard yellow cheese which is used either as table cheese or grated on various dishes.

Pancakes

- 1 cup water
- ½ teaspoon salt
- 1 tbsp lemon juice
- 1 cup flour
- ½ cup grape juice syrup or honey or sugar
  ground cinnamon
  chopped walnuts or sesame seeds

Mix water with salt, lemon juice and flour to achieve a thick batter.
Heat olive oil in a frying pan. Drop spoon-size amounts of the batter into the pan. Fry both sides and then place on kitchen roll in order to drain.
Transfer on a plate and pour grape juice syrup or honey diluted with 2-3

spoons of water over them. Sprinkle with walnuts or sesame seeds and cinnamon. They can even be sprinkled with sugar. You can also add ½ cup of sour mizithra cheese or crumbled feta cheese to the flour mixture.

Small pies with greens

Dough:

- 1 cup water
- ½ teaspoon salt
- 3 tbsps olive oil
- 1 tbsp lemon juice
- ½ kg flour

Filling:
- 1 kg greens
  (spinach, fennel,
  mint, parsley,
  leeks, spring onions)
- ½ cup olive oil
  salt, pepper

Prepare the filling: Wash and finely chop the greens. Put olive oil in a pan, heat it and sauté the greens for 10 minutes, adding a little water if needed. Season with salt and pepper and leave in a colander to strain. (They may need quite a few hours, therefore you'd better prepare them the day before and keep refrigerated).

Prepare the dough: Use the above ingredients and knead until you obtain hard dough. Cover and refrigerate for an hour.

Roll out the dough to 2mm thickness, cut out circles the size of a small saucer and fill its one with a teaspoon of the filling. Fold each circle in two and press down the edges with the prongs of a fork. Fry in very hot olive oil.

Tomato keftethes

- 3 medium-size ripe tomatoes,
  seeded and finely chopped
- 1 grated medium onion
- 1 teaspoon salt
- ½ teaspoon pepper
- 1 teaspoon dried rubbed
  oregano
- 1 tbsp parsley or mint,
  finely chopped
- 1 cup self-rising flour
  olive oil for frying

In a large bowl, put onion, tomatoes, oregano, parsley or mint, salt and freshly ground pepper. Add flour and knead until the ingredients are well combined and have the consistency of a thick batter.

Heat olive oil in a frying pan and when it's ready take tablespoons of the batter and drop carefully into the pan. Fry on both sides until golden brown. Dry on kitchen roll and serve immediately. One egg, 3 tbsps cheese and one more tbsp flour can be added to the batter, if desired.

Courgette keftedes

1   kg courgettes
2   grated medium-size onions
2   eggs
1   cup finely chopped parsley
½   cup grated cheese
½   cup ground toasted bread
    salt and pepper
    flour and olive oil, for frying

Wash courgettes, grate them and place into a colander with 1 tbsp salt to drain completely. For better results, place grated courgettes in a piece of cloth and squeeze off all liquid. In a large bowl, mix courgettes, parsley, onions, beaten eggs, cheese, pepper and toasted bread. Knead well until the mixture is as thick as a paste, adding more bread if needed. Heat olive oil in a frying pan until it almost smokes. Take heaping table-spoons of the mixture, shape into patties, dredge with flour and fry on both sides until golden brown. Dry on kitchen roll and serve.

Spinach pancakes

1   kg spinach
2   medium dried onions or 5-6 spring onions
½   cup finely chopped dill
½   cup finely chopped parsley
    salt and pepper
1   cup self-rising flour
    olive oil for frying

Wash spinach and put it in boiling water for 5 minutes. Drain and chop it finely. In a large bowl, mix spinach, onions, dill, parsley, salt and pepper. Make a thick batter with 1 cup flour and 1 cup water and add to the mixture. Combine well, adding a little more salt, if needed. Heat olive oil in a frying pan almost to the point of smoking and put in tablespoons of the spinach mixture. Fry on both sides until golden brown. Dry on kitchen roll.

Scrambled eggs

- 2 finely chopped green peppers
- 2 finely chopped onions
- 3 grated ripe tomatoes
- 5 eggs
- ½ cup crumbled feta cheese or any other cheese
- 1 teaspoon dried rubbed oregano
  salt and pepper
- 4 tbsps olive oil

Heat olive oil in a skillet over medium heat and soften onions and peppers. Add tomatoes and simmer until almost all liquid has evaporated, stirring occasionally.
Break the eggs and put into the skillet one at a time stirring with a wooden spoon until they are cooked and combined with the rest of the ingredients in the skillet. Add cheese, salt, pepper and oregano and cook for a further 5 minutes, stirring often until liquid is cooked off. Serve warm.

Fried fish with vinegar (savore)

1 kg medium-size fish (red mullet, smelt, horse-mackerel etc) or large fish cut into thick slices
salt, pepper
juice of 1 lemon
1 cup flour
olive oil for frying

For the sauce:
4 tbsps olive oil
3 tbsps vinegar
3 tbsps water
2 tbsps rosemary, either dried or fresh, 1 tbsp flour
2-3 cloves garlic (optional)

Clean, gut and wash fish, baste with lemon juice and salt and refrigerate for a couple of hours. Heat olive oil in a frying pan almost to the smoking point, dredge fish with flour and fry on both sides until golden brown and crispy. Place in a serving tray. In another pan, heat 4 tbsps olive oil and slightly brown garlic. Remove it and add one tbsp flour. Stir constantly with a wooden spoon until it gains a little colour and then put in vinegar, water, rosemary, a little salt and pepper. Simmer for 2-3 minutes and pour over the fried fish. Turn the fish on the other side after a few hours. The fish which are used for this recipe have a thin skin and can be soaked in the vinegar. For this reason they can be kept in the fridge in the marinade for quite a few days. Tomato can be added to the above marinade, if desired.

Fried mussels

1 kg mussels
olive oil, for frying

For the batter:
½ cup flour
1 egg
1 teaspoon salt
½ teaspoon baking soda
1 cup beer or water

For the yoghurt dip:
300 grams strained yoghurt
3 mashed garlic cloves
2 tbsps vinegar or lemon juice
2 tbsps olive oil
salt and pepper
½ cup roughly ground walnuts

First prepare the yoghurt dip by combining yoghurt, garlic, salt, pepper, olive oil, vinegar or lemon juice and walnuts.

Prepare the mussels: Wash and remove the hairy edges.

Boil them in a large pot with enough water for 5 minutes until the mussels have opened. Discard those which have not opened, as they are dead.
Separate the mussels from their shells and sprinkle with salt and pepper.
Make a thick batter with the beer or water, beaten egg, salt, baking soda and flour.

Dip mussels, one at a time, in the batter and fry in very hot olive oil until golden brown on both sides. Drain on kitchen roll.

Place on a serving tray with yoghurt dip in the centre.

Omelet with boiled potatoes

2   medium-size potatoes
4   eggs
1   tbsp finely chopped mint
     salt and pepper
2   tbsps grated cheese
2   tbsps olive oil

Boil the potatoes or cook under the grill. (You can use boiled or grilled potatoes which have been left over).
Peel them and mash slightly with a fork. Mix with beaten eggs, cheese,

mint, salt and pepper.
Heat 2 tbsps olive oil in a frying pan and pour the mixture into it. Cook for 5-6 minutes and carefully flip omelet to cook on the other side.

Fried pumpkin

  1   kg pumpkin in slices 2 cm thick
  1   teaspoon salt
  1   cup flour
      olive oil, for frying
  3   tbsps lemon juice or vinegar

Season pumpkin slices with salt and place into a colander to drain.
Heat olive oil in a frying pan almost to smoking point. Dredge pumpkin with flour and put into the hot oil. Fry over high heat on both sides until golden brown and crispy.
Serve immediately sprinkled with lemon juice. If you prefer vinegar then you have to proceed as following: After frying the pumpkin, discard olive oil leaving 1/3 of it. Add carefully 3 tbps vinegar into the hot olive oil and pour this blend over the fried pumpkin.

Fried vegetables
with yoghurt or tomato sauce

  2   aubergines
  4   courgettes
  4   green peppers
      salt
      olive oil for frying

For the batter:

  1   cup beer
  1   cup flour
  1   tbsp olive oil
      salt, pepper

For the tomato sauce:
2 tbsps olive oil
1 large onion sliced into rings
½ kg peeled, seeded and chopped tomatoes
2 finely chopped garlic cloves
2 tbsps vinegar
   salt, pepper
For the yoghurt dip:
½ kg strained yoghurt
2 mashed garlic cloves
½ teaspoon salt

Wash aubergines, remove stems and cut into 1 cm slices. Sprinkle with salt and put aside for half an hour. Do the same with courgettes, only cut them into thinner slices. Wash peppers, remove stems and seeds, cut into two and sprinkle with salt.
Mix beer, olive oil, salt, pepper and flour and make a thick batter.
Heat olive oil in a frying pan, dry aubergine and courgette slices, dip in the batter and deep fry until golden brown on both sides. Drain on kitchen roll.
Deep fry peppers and put in a serving tray. Place courgettes and aubergines on top of peppers.

Serve fried vegetables with yoghurt which has been combined with garlic and a little salt or with the tomato sauce which is made as follows: Sauté the onion in olive oil in a pan, add tomatoes, garlic, vinegar, salt and pepper. Cook until the sauce thickens.

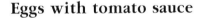

Eggs with tomato sauce

1   medium-size onion,
    finely chopped
1   bell pepper, finely
    chopped
2   tbsps olive oil
2   tomatoes, peeled,
    seeded and chopped
    salt, pepper
2   tbsps grated cheese
    (optional)
2   eggs

Fry onion and pepper in olive oil until soft. Add tomatoes, salt and pepper and when the sauce thickens, stir in cheese. Break the eggs in the sauce, sprinkle with a little salt and fry until the egg whites are cooked.

ONLY OLIVE OIL IN SALADS

Extra virgin olive oil, the natural juice of the olive, is the oil which should never be left out of salads. On Crete, an area with a high production of olive oil, salads swim –well almost- in olive oil and this seems strange to visitors who are not used to this.

Extra virgin olive oil offers the chance of extremely healthy combinations, especially when the salads use fresh vegetables and greens, as is used in the traditional Greek diet. Again, it is Crete that gives a true example for life. The Cretans prefer to eat their own fresh vegetables and the bountiful greens which the earth produces unaided, without being cooked. In nearly all the traditional salads there is the combination of extra virgin olive oil with various greens and vegetables.

Greek salad with olives

2   firm tomatoes
2   cucumbers
1   medium-size onion
½   cup purslane
½   cup parsley
1   green pepper
1   tbsp pickled capers
5-6 black olives
½   teaspoon salt
100 grams feta cheese
1   teaspoon oregano
4   tbsps olive oil
1   tbsp vinegar

Wash tomatoes, cucumbers, parsley, green pepper and purslane. Cut all of them into pieces and put in a salad bowl. Add capers, onion cut into thin rings and olives. Season with salt and oregano, pour over the dressing with olive oil and vinegar and mix. At the end place feta cheese on top of the salad.

Salad with dried rusks

On Crete they are used to eating dried rusks, bread which had been in the oven, (for quite a few hours at very low temperature) for a second time and had been dried out. In the old days, this was the easiest way of preserving bread by the farmers as it wasn't possible to cook fresh bread every day. Many types of dried rusks in various shapes can be found in Greece, whether rectangular, square or circular and also dried rusks made with a range of ingredients and with different ways of preparation (rusks made with whole wheat, with barley flour, with a mixture of wheat and barley, with chick peas etc.). These rusks are hard, thick, toasted slices of bread which are softened with water or olive oil and then eaten. Shops in Europe and America which sell Greek products have these dried rusks and the best are from Crete.

The following salad is a traditional one in the area of Mylopotamos on Crete.

- 2 barley or wheat paximathia (rusks)
- 2 firm tomatoes
- 2 cucumbers
- 1 medium onion
- 1 bell pepper
- 5-6 black olives
- ½ teaspoon salt
- 100 grams feta cheese
- 1 teaspoon dried oregano
- 4 tbsps olive oil or according to desire taste

In a salad bowl, place the rusks broken into chunks and dampen slightly with 2 tbsps olive oil. Wash tomatoes, cucumber and pepper.

Chop them into pieces and put on the rusks. Add the roughly chopped onion and olives. Season with salt and oregano, drizzle with remaining oil (or more) and mix. Finally, add the feta cheese in crumbs.

Bulgur salad

1   cup bulgur (wheat which has been boiled and then ground)
1   finely chopped large dried onion or 5-6 spring onions
2   tomatoes, seeded and chopped
2   tbsps finely chopped parsley
1   tbsp finely chopped mint (optional)
4   tbsps olive oil, 2 tbsps vinegar
    salt, ½ mashed hot pepper

Soak bulgur in warm water for one hour and drain well. Add remaining ingredients and mix well.

Salad with "rocket" and tomatoes

2   firm tomatoes, cut into wedges
1   cup roughly chopped "rocket"
10 olives
½   teaspoon salt pepper
3   tbsps olive oil
1   tbsp vinegar

Place in a salad bowl the tomatoes, rocket and olives. Make a dressing by shaking well olive oil, vinegar, salt and pepper and pour over the salad.

Salad with apples and walnuts

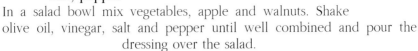

1	cup grated carrot
1	cup grated cabbage
1	cup grated beetroot
1	cup grated apple
½	cup roughly ground walnuts
4	tbsps olive oil
4	tbsps lemon juice
	salt, pepper

In a salad bowl mix vegetables, apple and walnuts. Shake olive oil, vinegar, salt and pepper until well combined and pour the dressing over the salad.

Purslane
with yoghurt and walnuts

Purslane is a self-sown plant in many countries, but usually it is regarded as a weed in gardens. On Crete, which has given many lessons on a healthy diet, purslane is not considered a weed. On the con-

trary, it is cultivated as it is eaten regularly in salads. You can grow purslane even in plant pots where it will thrive for years! Purslane has a large quantity of Omega 3 fats, which is believed to be a shield of protection for the heart.

½   kg purslane
3   tbsps olive oil
250 grams strained yoghurt
2   mashed garlic cloves
1   tbsp vinegar or lemon juice
½   teaspoon salt
2   tbsps roughly chopped walnuts

Wash and clean purslane, discarding the thick sprigs. Put it in a salad bowl.
Combine well yoghurt with garlic, olive oil, vinegar or lemon juice, salt and walnuts. Pour over purslane and mix.

Dried bean salad

1   cup dried beans
1   medium onion cut into slices
2   green peppers cut into slices
3   tomatoes, peeled, seeded and chopped
3   tbsps finely chopped parsley
1   tbsp finely chopped basil (optional)
4   tbsps olive oil
2   tbsps vinegar or lemon juice
    salt
10 black olives
2   boiled eggs

Boil the beans in water until they are soft but not overcooked and then drain. (They can be soaked in water for a few hours prior to cooking).
In a salad bowl, mix beans with onion, peppers, tomatoes and parsley. Whisk olive oil with salt and vinegar or lemon juice and pour over the salad. Garnish with olives and slices of boiled eggs.
The salad is quite delicious by just adding finely chopped onion and dill and a dressing with olive oil and lemon juice.

OLIVE OIL IN PULSES

In the traditional diet of Crete, pulses play a leading role, one which is detected in the finds of archaeological and palaeobotanic researches. Since prehistoric times, the inhabitants of Crete but also the Aegean in general have used pulses on a regular basis in their diet. Panspermia, the offering to the gods of a small amount of all the grains, was an important expression of thanks by the ancient Greeks but also a ritual ceremony for vegetation and renewal of life.

Greek mythology has documented the importance of pulses as ritual dishes, stating that this was Deucalion and Pyrrha's first food after the flood which destroyed mankind. When the downpour stopped and the floods ebbed, the two mythological founders of mankind were to be found on earth alone and without food. The only thing that had remained was a few seeds of all kinds. They boiled these altogether and ate them with mixed feelings. On the one hand, they felt the joy of being saved and on the other, the great loss of all the other people. It really was a meal of great joy and sorrow all mixed up! If we look again at the symbolism in this myth, then we will see that the circle of joy and sorrow is one and the same with the circle of life as it is with the seed: we bury it but it does not die, instead, it is reborn, growing and producing other seeds in the process!

In the nutritional culture, pulses are almost always consumed with olive oil. There are days when the Orthodox Church disallows the consumption of olive oil, but pulses, soaked in water for a few hours, are still eaten. These pulses are eaten with olives! "Vrechtokoukia", (broad beans which have been left a whole day in water to dampen and soften) are perfect and they are a main dish in Lent foods on Crete and the Aegean islands. In periods of religious fasting, in some monasteries they are used to cooking pulses with olives.

The science of nutrition heavily recommends that today, people should not abandon this food which has been so important for both the development of society and the maintenance of good health, as has happened in many western societies. Of course, it is recommended that these dishes should be eaten with olive oil! Olive oil, apart from offering a unique guarantee of health, completes the dishes which are prepared with pulses and produces a harmony of tastes. Traditional cooking offers various suggestions on the making of dishes based on pulses, such as pulses with vegetables or mashed pulses.

Split pea purée

Mediterranean fava is made with broad beans. Greek fava uses peeled and cracked seeds of the plant Lathyrus Sativus (yellow lentil). In other countries fava is usually to be found in Greek specialty shops. The dish which is made in the Greek way resembles a purée and is drizzled generously with extra virgin olive oil.

½   kg fava (yellow or green split peas)
2   medium onions, roughly chopped
1   teaspoon salt, pepper
3   tbsps olive oil

To serve:
    olive oil,
    according
    to taste
2   lemons in slices
1   finely chopped
    onion
    olives (optional)

Place split peas in a pot with onion, salt, 3 tbsps olive oil and cover with 5 cups water. Cook over low heat until it becomes a mush and nearly all the water has been boiled off, about one hour. The pot should not be covered because the fava expands and so it might spill over. Near the end, stir continuously so that it doesn't stick to the bottom of the pot and also to help it turn into a pulp. When it cools, it becomes thicker. On serving, add olive oil according to taste, finely chopped onion, lemon slices, olives, capers or mint leaves, if so desired. The dish served should first be rubbed with garlic.

Mixed pulses
(Pallikaria or polysporia)

A traditional dish known throughout nearly all of Greece. In the old days it was made on special occasions (the celebration of the Virgin Mary on 21st November, St Andrew on 30th November etc). Farmers believed that with this dish they helped the good production of cereal crops. It is a survival of ancient Greek customs and, more precisely, of "Thargilia". Then, they boiled crop produce in a pot and offered to the gods. Today in Greece, it is a tasty salad but also a delicious and wholesome soup.

100 grams of each type of pulses (wheat, chick peas, beans, broad beans, lentils etc)
salt, pepper
To serve: fresh or dried onion, dill, olive oil, lemon juice

Soak the pulses the night before. Wheat and chickpeas need more time in cooking, therefore place in separate bowls. Lentils do not need to be soaked at all. The next day, rinse the pulses and place wheat first in a large pot. Cover with enough water and boil for 30 minutes. Add chick peas and cook for another 15 minutes. Add remaining pulses and continue cooking until soft. Season with salt and pepper and serve either as a soup in its own juices or drained as a salad, in both cases drizzled with olive oil and lemon juice and sprinkled with finely chopped onion and dill, to desired taste.

Lentil soup

½   kg lentils (brown)
1   medium onion, finely chopped
½   cup olive oil
2-3 finely chopped garlic cloves
1   tbsp tomato paste or 3 ripe grated tomatoes
3   laurel leaves
    salt, pepper
3   tbsps good quality vinegar

Place lentils in a pot with enough water to cover them and boil for 5-6 minutes., then drain them. Brown onion in olive oil, add the lentils, garlic, tomato paste diluted in 1 cup water or just the tomatoes, laurel leaves, salt, pepper and water to cover. Boil the lentils until cooked which will take about half an hour. Add vinegar, boil for 5 more minutes and the dish is ready.

Black-eyed beans with fennel

½   kg black-eyed beans
½   cup olive oil
1   medium onion, finely chopped
300 grams finely chopped fennel
1   tbsp tomato paste or ½ kg grated tomatoes
     salt and pepper, to taste

Put the beans in a pot, cover well with water and boil for half an hour to half-cook. Transfer the beans into a colander to drain. Put olive oil, onion and fennel in the pot and sauté for 5 minutes. Add 2-3 cups water and cook for 15 minutes, then add tomato paste diluted in 1 cup water or the tomatoes, salt and pepper. Allow fennel to slowly simmer and almost cook, at which point add the beans, along with more water to cover and leave to cook completely.

Chick pea keftethes

½   kg chick peas
1   grated medium-sized onion
2   egg yolks
4   tbsps of ground dried
     rusk or toasted bread
½   cup finely chopped
     parsley
     salt, pepper
½   cup grated cheese
     (optional)
     flour, olive oil for
     frying

Soak chick peas overnight and
the next day drain and rub them
to remove husks. Rinse with cold
water and then boil them in a pot until
soft. Drain again and place in a food processor
along with 2-3 tbsps of the water from boiling. Grind for 2-3 minutes, add the other ingredients and grind to combine them well. Taking a tablespoon of mixture at a time, shape into croquettes. Dredge in flour and fry them in olive oil. Serve alone or with tomato sauce. In the same way we can make croquettes with split peas or with different pulses together (dried beans, broad beans, chick peas and split peas).

Spaniatha

Basic but special food with Byzantine roots. Byzantine texts refer to "aghiozoumi", holy juice from water, oil and aromatics plants, which were boiled together and served on plates, poured over slices of bread which had been placed on them. From this dish, come various country dishes which are still made in Greece, such as "panatha", a simple and basic meal. "Spaniatha" is linked to the Asterousia, the mountains in southern Crete and shows a different version of the Byzantine dish.

300	grams dried beans
5	tbsps olive oil
1	medium onion in slices
	salt, pepper
	dried rusks

In a pot with enough water, boil the beans until cooked, making sure that some juice is left.

Brown the onion in olive oil in a pan until it changes colour. Add beans with their juice, salt and pepper and cook for 10 minutes.

Serve in a dish with a dried rusk underneath the beans. (It is optional to add lemon juice).

PASTAS AND OLIVE OIL

Mussels pilaf

    1   kg mussels
    2   cups rice
    4-5 tbsps olive oil
    2   medium onions, finely chopped
    100 ml white wine
    2   medium tomatoes, seeded and mashed
         salt and pepper to taste

Prepare the mussels: Wash and scrub them very well and remove the hairy edges.

Boil them in a large pot with enough water for 5 minutes until the mussels have opened. Discard those which have not opened, as they are dead. Separate the mussels from their shells and leave them aside.

Heat oil in a large pot and soften onions for 3-4 minutes. Add mussels and, after a while, the rice and stir for another 4 minutes. Pour in wine, tomatoes and 5 cups water and keep cooking on medium heat until almost all liquid has been absorbed, about 15 minutes. Season with salt and pepper, stir for another minute and remove from heat. Cover with a clean towel until served.

Bread with Garlic and Olive oil

5   slices of bread
3   tbsps olive oil, flavoured with garlic

Toast bread slices under the grill or on barbecue fire and, when still hot, drizzle garlic-flavoured olive oil and serve immediately.

Stuffed Courgette Flowers

40 courgette flowers
½   kg ripe tomatoes, seeded and mashed
2   onions, finely chopped
2   tbsps parsley, finely chopped
½   kg rice
    salt and pepper to taste
3/4 cup olive oil

Buy or pick the courgette flowers in the morning when they are wide open. Place them upright in a bowl soaking the stems, not the flowers, to keep them open until you need them. When you are ready, wash them carefully because they tear easily and remove the stems from inside. Prepare the stuffing: In a large bowl mix rice, onions, ½ cup olive oil, tomatoes, parsley, 1 cup water, salt and pepper. (You can substitute half the rice to the same quantity of minced meat). Pour remaining oil in a pot. Take one courgette flower at a time and carefully fill with 1 tbsp rice stuffing. Fold the top of the flower over to close it and place each flower in the pot. Place a plate over the dolmathes to keep them from opening, pour enough water to almost cover them and simmer for about 50 minutes, until almost all liquid has been absorbed.

Ground wheat pilaf with tomato sauce

½   kg chondros or bulgur (chondros is roughly ground wheat while bulgur is wheat which has been first boiled and then ground)
½   cup olive oil
2   medium onions, finely chopped
2   courgettes, finely chopped
1   medium potato, finely chopped
½   kg ripe tomatoes, peeled, seeded and chopped
    salt and pepper to taste
6   cups water or meat stock

Wash and drain chondros or bulgur: Put it in a large bowl with hot water to cover it, add 2 tbsps salt and when water gets cold place chondros or bulgur in a colander and rinse it thoroughly. In a pot heat olive oil and soften onions until translucent. Add courgettes, potato and tomatoes and stir for 5 minutes. Pour 6 cups water or meat stock and when it comes to the boil, add the chondros or bulgur. (The ratio of water to bulgur should be 2:1). Reduce heat to low and simmer until the water is absorbed and the chondros soft, about 20 minutes, stirring often to prevent it from sticking to the bottom of the pot. Serve sprinkled with grated cheese, if desired.

Aubergine pilaf

½   kg aubergines
½   cup olive oil for frying
2   medium onions, finely chopped
2   tbsps olive oil
3   medium ripe tomatoes, peeled, seeded and chopped
1   cup rice
   salt and black pepper

Wash aubergines, remove stems, cut into dice, sprinkle with salt and let them stand for half an hour. Wash and drain rice: Put it in a large bowl with hot water to cover it, add 2 tbsps salt and when water goes cold place rice in a colander and rinse it thoroughly under the tap. Dry diced aubergines, fry lightly in olive oil and place on kitchen roll. In a pot heat 2 tbsps olive oil, brown onions for 3 minutes, add rice and stir for 5 minutes. Add tomatoes, salt pepper, fried aubergines, 2,5 cups warm water and cook on moderate heat until all liquid has been absorbed, about 20 minutes.

Artichoke pilaf

5   artichoke hearts cut into cubes
3-4 tbsps olive oil
5-6 spring onions, finely chopped
3   medium-size carrots, cut into cubes
3   tbsps dill, finely chopped
1   cup rice
   salt and black pepper
   juice of 1 lemon

Prepare the artichokes: Remove the leaves and trim them very well leaving only the fleshy middle part, the heart. Rub with lemon and put them aside. Wash and drain rice as above. Heat olive oil in a large pot and add spring onions, carrots, diced artichokes and dill. Stir for 8-10 minutes until juice has evaporated and add rice. Stir a couple of times with a wooden spoon and then pour in 2,5 cups warm water, season with salt and pepper and cook on moderate heat until liquid has been absorbed. Remove pot from heat, pour in lemon juice, give a good stir and cover pot with a clean towel for a quarter of an hour before it's served.

MEAT - FISH WITH OLIVE OIL

MChourmouzis – Vyzantius came to Crete from Constantinople at the beginning of 19th century. A phrase expressed by him, "they cook even pork with olive oil", shows the great importance of the precious juice of olives in a unique manner. Various foreign travellers to Crete but also groups of doctors who studied the dietary habits of the Cretans were equally surprised. This fact is almost inconceivable to the inhabitants of northern regions or northern countries because they use animal fat in cooking such dishes. Maybe that was similarly inconceivable to Cretans who ""are used to cooking with olive oil", as the learned British traveller Robert Pashley wrote in 1834.

The American members of the Rockefeller Foundation who carried out a study in 1948, observed the dietary habits of the inhabitants of the island and pointed out that "at noon they eat vegetables, pulses or starches".

On the island of Crete, where the diet of the people is believed to be the healthiest in the world and certainly the model of the Mediterranean diet, meat is consumed usually cooked with wild edible greens, vegetables and pulses. Even the formal Easter dish is lamb or goat with seasonal vegetables (wild greens, lettuce or artichokes…) cooked with olive oil, of course!

Olive oil gives a special taste to meat or fish dishes, makes them lighter and healthier.

Grilled meat with olive oil and oregano

1,5	kg meat (any kind of meat)
½	cup olive oil
	juice of 2 lemons
1	teaspoon salt

Wash meat, cut into serving portions, put in a large bowl and add olive oil, lemon juice, salt and oregano. Let it marinate for at least 4 hours, turning it on all sides to soak in the marinade.

Grill the meat on barbecue fire, basting it from time to time with the marinade until soft and brown.

Pork or lamb with prunes

- 1.5   kg meat (pork or lamb)
- 1   medium onion, finely chopped
-       salt, pepper, a little nutmeg
- 1   cinnamon stick
- 5-6   whole cloves
-       juice of 2 lemons
- 3-4   tbsps olive oil
- ½   kg pitted prunes
- ½   cup almonds
- 2   tbsps sugar or honey

Wash meat and cut into cubes.

Place it in a large bowl and add onion, salt, pepper, nutmeg, cinnamon, cloves and lemon juice. Allow it to marinate for at least 1 hour.

In the meantime soak prunes in water. Soak almonds in hot water, peel, roast and put aside.

Heat olive oil in a large pot, add meat and cook until juice has evaporated. Pour in marinade along with 1-2 cups lukewarm water and simmer until meat is soft enough, about one hour. Add prunes, almonds and sugar or honey and continue cooking for 10 more minutes. Serve warm.

Pork with potatoes and coriander

1   kg boneless pork
4   medium potatoes
4-5 tbsps olive oil
4   cloves of garlic, finely chopped
3/4 cup red wine
2   tbsps coriander
     salt and black pepper

Cut meat in cubes, wash and place in a large bowl. Make marinade by combining garlic, wine, coriander, salt and pepper. Pour over meat, cover and put the bowl in a cool place for at least 4 hours. Turn the meat pieces on all sides from time to time to marinate fully.
Heat olive oil in a saucepan. Remove meat from marinade with a slotted spoon and put in the pot turning frequently to brown lightly. Add marinade to pot, reduce fire and simmer until half done, adding water if needed. Add potatoes peeled, washed and quartered, a little salt and continue cooking for about half an hour, adding more water again, if needed.

Veal with spaghetti

1   kg veal
1   large onion, finely chopped
5   tbsps olive oil
3   cloves of garlic, coarsely chopped
100 ml white wine
1   kg ripe tomatoes, peeled,
     seeded and chopped
1   cinnamon stick
5-6 cloves, 2-3 bay leaves
     salt, pepper
½   kg spaghetti No 5
1   cup grated cheese

Wash meat, cut into cubes and dry.
In a large pot heat olive oil and add meat. Cook turning on all sides on moderate heat until juice is evaporated. Stir in wine, garlic, tomatoes, cinnamon, cloves, bay leaves, salt, pepper, 1-2 cups water and simmer until meat is soft enough, about one and a half hours.
In another large pot put in water, one teaspoon salt and bring to the boil. Add spaghetti and boil for 15 minutes over high heat. Transfer spaghetti into a colander and rinse with cold water.
Serve spaghetti topped with meat and sauce and sprinkled with grated cheese.

Chicken in wine

1   medium-size chicken
½   cup olive oil
2   medium onions, finely chopped
3   cloves of garlic, coarsely chopped
2   cups red wine
½   kg ripe tomatoes, peeled, seeded and chopped
    salt and pepper to taste

Cut chicken into serving pieces, wash well and pat dry with kitchen roll. In a large stewing pot, heat olive oil and brown onion for 3 minutes. Continue with meat until juice is evaporated, turning frequently on all sides. Add garlic, wine and 2 cups warm water and simmer till meat is half cooked. Add tomatoes, salt and pepper and continue cooking for another 30 minutes.
Serve with plain rice, with roasted or fried potatoes or with noodles.

Bream with celery

1   kg medium size bream fish
1   kg coarsely chopped celery
2   medium onions, finely chopped
½   cup olive oil
    salt and pepper
2   eggs
    juice of 2 lemons

Clean, gut and wash fish. Season with salt and keep in the fridge.
Wash celery and put in large pot with boiling water for 5 minutes. Drain and leave aside.
In a saucepan heat olive oil, brown onions for 3-4 minutes and add celery, salt and pepper. Cover with warm water and simmer for about 25-30 minutes.
Place the fish on top of celery and continue simmering for 20 more minutes, without stirring but just shaking the pot from time to time to prevent food from sticking to the bottom of the pot.
When food has been cooked, prepare the egg and lemon sauce: Beat the eggs (first the whites and then the yolks) with the lemon juice until frothy. Add a few ladles of liquid from the pot beating constantly until the egg and lemon mixture is warm. Remove pot from heat, pour in the egg mixture and stir well.

Baked Mackerel with raisins and walnuts

1,5 kg mackerel fish or trout
2   medium onions, finely chopped
2-3 garlic cloves, finely chopped
5   tbsps olive oil
½   kg tomatoes peeled, seeded and chopped
½   cup seedless raisins, soaked in water for 30 minutes
½   cup coarsely ground walnuts
    salt, pepper

Clean mackerel, remove guts, season with salt and place in a baking tray in one layer.
Combine tomatoes, onions, garlic, raisins, walnuts, salt and pepper and stuff the fish with this mixture. Spread the rest of the mixture on top of the fish, drizzle olive oil and bake for 50-60 minutes.

Cod with potatoes in lemon sauce

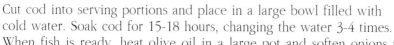

1   kg salted cod (preferably filleted)
or fresh cod
1   kg potatoes
½   cup olive oil
1   large onion, finely chopped
3   garlic cloves, finely chopped
3   tbsps lemon juice, pepper

Cut cod into serving portions and place in a large bowl filled with cold water. Soak cod for 15-18 hours, changing the water 3-4 times. When fish is ready, heat olive oil in a large pot and soften onions until they gain a little colour. Add potatoes peeled and cut into quarters, garlic and 2 cups water and simmer for 15 minutes. Place cod on top of the potatoes and cook gently for a further 20 minutes, shaking the pot from time to time. Five minutes before food is ready pour lemon juice over the food and shake the pot.

If you prefer a thicker sauce you can dilute one tbsp of flour in a little water and add it to the pot along with the lemon juice.

Baked fish with vegetables and rosemary

1   big whole fish (grouper, red snapper, pike, sea bream, mullet)
3   sun dried tomatoes
2-3   bay leaves
3   tbsps finely chopped parsley
3-4   medium onions, sliced into thin rings
2   finely chopped garlic cloves
4   tbsps olive oil
100   ml white wine
3   medium tomatoes peeled,
seeded and chopped
       salt, pepper
1   teaspoon rosemary
½   cup black olives (optional)

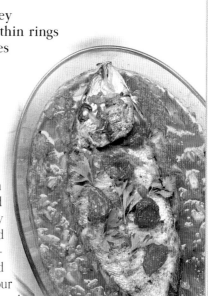

Clean fish, remove guts and stuff with parsley, bay leaves and sun dried tomatoes. Place in an oiled baking tray in one layer. In a saucepan heat oil and brown onions lightly. Add garlic, tomatoes, wine, rosemary, olives, salt and pepper and simmer for 5 minutes. Pour the sauce over and around the fish and bake in moderate heat for about an hour.

Baked Fish with bell peppers

1   big whole fish (pike, red snapper, mullet, monkfish)
3   tbsps finely chopped parsley
2   medium onions, sliced into thin rings
2   finely chopped garlic cloves
½   kg peeled, seeded and chopped tomatoes
½   kg bell peppers, sliced into rings
6   tbsps olive oil
100 ml white wine
    salt, pepper
    juice of 1 lemon

Combine onions, peppers, tomatoes and garlic and place in an oiled baking tray.
Clean fish, remove guts, stuff with parsley and place on top of the sauce. Season with salt, drizzle with olive oil, wine and lemon juice and bake in moderate heat for about one hour.

Fish Soup (Kakavia)

This is the favourite soup of the Greek fishermen but also of the inhabitants of the islands and coastal areas of Greece. It can be prepared in various manners, but fishermen used to make it very simply, with only sea water, without, of course, adding any salt. Having its origin in Greek antiquity, it took its name from the pot in which it was cooked in Byzantine years, the kakavi. The very well known bouillabaisse of Marseilles is believed to have evolved from this Greek fish soup.

- 1,5 kg whole fish (bass, cod, red snapper, pike, grouper)
- 4 tbsps of olive oil
- 2 onions, sliced into thin rings
- 5-6 medium potatoes, peeled and cut into quarters
- salt, pepper
- juice of 2 lemons
- 1,5 litre water

Scrape and wash fish and remove guts. Cut into large slices. In a soup pot heat olive oil and soften onions until lightly brown. Add potatoes and cover with enough water. Boil for 10 minutes, then add fish, salt and pepper and continue cooking for a further 25-30 minutes. Remove pot from heat and pour in lemon juice.

Meat with spinach in tomato sauce

- 1 kg meat (lamb or veal)
- 1 kg spinach
- 6 tbsps olive oil
- 2 medium onions, finely chopped
- ½ kg tomatoes peeled, seeded and chopped
- salt and pepper to taste

Wash meat and cut into cubes.
Heat the oil in a saucepan and soften the onions until they take on a little colour. Add meat and turn a few times on all sides to colour evenly. Stir in tomatoes, one cup water and cook gently for about 50 minutes.
In the meantime wash and chop spinach.
When meat is almost cooked, stir in spinach, salt and pepper and continue cooking until almost all liquid has been absorbed.

Roasted lamb with tomato sauce

1   kg lamb
1   kg potatoes, peeled and cut into quarters
½   kg tomatoes, cut into slices
    juice of 1 lemon
6   tbsps olive oil
2-3 bay leaves
    salt and pepper to taste

Wash meat, cut into serving pieces, dry and baste with lemon juice. Place in a baking tray, season with salt, pepper and 3 tbsps olive oil.
Place potatoes all around meat, season again with salt and pepper, place bay leaves among potatoes and drizzle remaining olive oil.
Top with tomato slices, pour in ½ cup water and bake in moderate heat for about an hour and a half, turning the meat over half way through.

Meat balls with potatoes in the oven

½   kg minced meat (lamb and veal or pork)
1   egg, beaten
2   medium onions, grated
2   mashed garlic cloves
2   slices of stale bread, soaked in water and squeezed dry
3   tbsps finely chopped parsley
½   kg tomatoes peeled, seeded and chopped
1   bell pepper, finely chopped
1   teaspoon dried thyme
6   medium potatoes
    salt and pepper
4   tbsps olive oil

In a large bowl mix and knead minced meat, 1 onion, garlic, egg, parsley, bell pepper, bread, thyme, salt and pepper punching the mixture with your knuckles.
Peel potatoes, cut into round slices, season with salt and pepper and place in an oiled baking tray.
Take small portions of the minced meat mixture, shape into balls and gently flatten them. Place on top of potatoes.
Heat olive oil in a pan and brown the other onion for 3 minutes. Stir in tomatoes, one cup water, salt and pepper and simmer for 5 minutes. Top with sauce and bake in moderate heat for 25- 30 minutes. Turn meatballs on the other side and continue cooking for another 20 minutes.

Beef stew

1 kg beef
6 tbsps olive oil
½ kg pearl onions or large onions sliced into thin rings
3 garlic cloves
2 tbsps vinegar
  salt, pepper
1 teaspoon pimento
1 cinnamon stick

Wash meat and cut into cubes.
Heat olive oil in a saucepan, add meat and cook on medium heat until juice is evaporated. Add onions and peeled whole cloves of garlic and soften for 5 minutes. Stir in vinegar, salt, pepper, pimento, cinnamon and 3 cups warm water. Cover and simmer for 2 hours, until meat is tender.

Rabbit with walnuts

1 medium-size rabbit
½ cup olive oil
3 onions, sliced into thin rings
½ cup white wine
  salt
½ cup coarsely ground walnuts

For the marinade:

1,5 cup white wine
1 cup celery root sliced into rings
2 carrots sliced into rings
2 cloves of garlic, peeled but whole
1 cinnamon stick, 5-6 whole cloves
2-3 bay leaves
2 onions, sliced into thin rings
5-6 peppercorns

Make marinade the evening before by combining the above ingredients. Wash and cut rabbit into serving pieces, place in a large bowl and cover with marinade.
The next day, heat olive oil in a saucepan and soften onions for 2-3 minutes until lightly brown. Remove rabbit pieces from marinade and add to the pan. Brown for 10 minutes until juice is evaporated and stir in ½ cup wine. Add walnuts and salt and simmer until rabbit is tender, about 40-45 minutes.

Baked pilchard or sardines with olive oil and oregano

1   kg pilchard or sardines
2   large onions, sliced into thin rings
    salt, pepper
4   tbsps olive oil
5   tbsps lemon juice
1   teaspoon oregano

Wash fish, remove heads and guts, season with salt and put into a colander to drain.

Place onions in an oiled baking tray or ovenproof dish and put fish on them. Whisk together olive oil, lemon juice, pepper and oregano and pour over fish. Bake in preheated oven for about 40 minutes until fish is lightly brown.

Dried beans with meat in the oven

1   kg meat (pork, veal or goat)
½   kg dried beans
2   medium onions, finely chopped
4   medium tomatoes, peeled, seeded and chopped
3   slices of sun dried tomatoes
2   finely chopped garlic cloves
½   cup olive oil
½   cup finely chopped parsley
1   chilli pepper (optional)
    salt, pepper

In a large pot put beans with enough water to cover them and boil for 10 minutes. Drain the beans.

Wash meat, cut into cubes and place in a baking tray. Add beans, onions, tomatoes, garlic, olive oil, parsley, chilli pepper, salt and freshly ground black pepper. Pour one litre water over beans, cover with aluminum foil and bake in moderate heat for about 2 hours. When food is almost ready, uncover the pan and bake for a further 15 minutes.

Meat with ground wheat in the oven

1	kg meat (pork, goat or lamb)
½	kg chondros (ground wheat)
1	medium onion, finely chopped
3	ripe tomatoes, seeded and grated
4-5	tbsps olive oil
	salt and pepper to taste

Wash and drain chondros: Put in a large bowl with hot water to cover it, add 2 tbsps salt and when water gets cold, place chondros in a colander and rinse thoroughly.

Wash meat, cut into cubes and place in a baking tray or ovenproof dish. Add chondros, onion, tomatoes, olive oil, salt and pepper. Pour 7 cups water or meat stock over chondros, cover pan with aluminum foil and bake in moderate heat for 2 hours. Near the end, uncover and bake for another 15 minutes.

Meat soup with vegetables

½	kg meat (lamb or veal)
4	tbsps olive oil
2	large onions, sliced into thin rings
2	celery roots sliced into 2 cm rings
2	leeks, sliced into rings
2	medium carrots, cut into cubes
3-4	medium potatoes, cut into cubes
	salt

Wash meat and cut into small cubes. Put in a soup pot with water to cover it. Add salt and bring to a slow boil skimming foam off top from time to time. Simmer until meat is almost ready.

In another saucepan heat olive oil, soften onions until they get a little colour and add celery, leeks, carrots and finally potatoes, stirring for 10-15 minutes. Season with salt and transfer into the pot with meat, add some more water if it is not enough, and continue cooking for another 15-20 minutes.

Lamb or goat with yoghurt

1   kg meat (lamb or goat)
½   kg strained yoghurt
4   tbsps olive oil
    salt

Wash meat and cut into medium pieces.
Place in a saucepan with olive oil and cook on low heat until tender. Top
with yoghurt, season with salt and cook for a further 15 minutes.

Mycenaean stew

*In summer 1999 an original exhibition took place in the National
Archaeological Museum, Athens. The title was "Minoan and Mycenaean
Tastes" and John Tzedakis was the head archaeologist. The researchers
displayed items and presented evidence (laboratory analyses) proving the
early use of olive oil in cooking by the inhabitants of Minoan Crete, even
before 2000 B.C. Among other documents they published a few indicative
recipes that might be close to the dietary habits of the Minoan or the
Mycenaean Greeks.*

1   kg pork
½   cup olive oil
1   kg coarsely chopped onions
2   finely chopped garlic cloves
2   bay leaves
2   cups wine
    salt, pepper, cumin

Wash meat and cut into cubes. Heat olive oil in a stewing pot and lightly
brown onions. Add bay leaves, garlic and meat. Cook until juice is
evaporated and then pour in wine. Season with salt, pepper, cumin,
reduce heat to low and simmer for 2 hours until meat is tender.

SUBSTITUTING MILK CREAM

The inventive Greeks have adjusted food products to their dietary needs or maybe they have adjusted those needs to the great variety of products! Nobody is surprised by the way animal fats are substituted by olive oil, which has been so favoured by recent dietary studies! The final taste is the result of the perfect balance of the ingredients used in the preparation of each dish.

In this chapter you will find a few such characteristic examples that prove that the use of olive oil in Greek cooking is a way of life!

Meat with potatoes and carrots in egg-lemon sauce

1   kg meat (lamb or veal)
4   tbsps olive oil
2   onions, sliced into thin rings
3   carrots, cut into sticks
1   kg potatoes, cut into quarters

2-3 bay leaves
1   teaspoon dried thyme
    salt, pepper
2   eggs
    juice of 2 lemons

Wash meat and cut into small pieces. Heat olive oil in a pot and soften onions until they get a little colour. Add meat and brown on all sides. Pour in enough water to cover meat and cook for 30-40 minutes until meat is half done. Add carrots, potatoes, bay leaves, salt and pepper and continue cooking for another 30 minutes.

Prepare egg and lemon sauce: Beat the eggs (first the whites and then the yolks) with the lemon juice until frothy.

Add a few ladles of the stock from the pot, beating constantly until the egg and lemon mixture is warm. Remove the pot from the heat, pour in the egg mixture and stir well.

Serve sprinkled with thyme.

Chicken with parsley in egg-lemon sauce

1   medium-size chicken
1   kg parsley
5-6 tbsps olive oil
5-6 spring onions coarsely chopped
      salt, pepper
2   eggs, juice of 2 lemons

Wash parsley and chop it coarsely. Wash chicken and cut into medium pieces. Heat olive oil in a saucepan and brown onions lightly. Add chicken and brown on all sides for 6-7 minutes. Put in parsley along with 3 cups water and cook for about one hour. When food is ready, season with salt and pepper and prepare the egg and lemon sauce (avgolemono): Beat the eggs (first the whites and then the yolks) with the lemon juice until frothy. Add a few ladles of the liquid from the pot, beating constantly until the egg and lemon mixture is warm. Remove pot from heat, pour in the egg mixture and shake the pot to mix the egg-lemon mixture with the food.
This recipe is also made with dill in place of parsley.

Lamb and artichokes in egg-lemon sauce

1	kg lamb
100	ml olive oil
1	medium onion or 3-4 spring onions, coarsely chopped
1/2	cup finely chopped dill
1	kg artichoke hearts
	salt, pepper
2	eggs
	juice of 2 lemons

Prepare the artichokes: Remove the leaves and trim them very well leaving only the fleshy middle part, the heart. Rub with lemon and put aside.

Wash meat and cut into pieces removing as much fat as you can.

Heat olive oil in a large pot, put in meat and brown on all sides for a few minutes. Add onion, dill, salt and pepper and 2 cups warm water. Simmer for about 40 minutes and then put in the artichokes. Cook for another 35 to 40 minutes adding more water if necessary.

Once the meat is done, prepare the egg and lemon sauce (avgolemono): Beat the eggs (first the whites and then the yolks) with the lemon juice until frothy. Add a few ladles of the stock from the pot, beating constantly until the egg and lemon mixture is warm. Remove pot from heat, pour in the egg mixture and shake the pot to mix the egg-lemon mixture with the food.

Chickpeas in flour-lemon sauce

½	kg chickpeas
½	cup olive oil
1	medium onion, finely chopped
	salt and pepper
1	tablespoon flour
	juice of 2 lemons

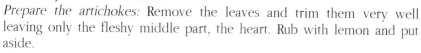

Soak chickpeas in water overnight. The next day, drain them and rub between your fingers to remove husks. Rinse with cold water.

Heat olive oil in a soup pot and soften onion. Add chickpeas and enough water to cover them and cook for about one hour and a half.

Dilute flour in lemon juice and a little liquid from the pot and pour over chickpeas. Season with salt and pepper to desired taste and stir well. Cook for 5 more minutes.

OLIVE OIL IN PIES

Pies are typical in the cuisine of northern Greece, but as olive oil is neither produced there nor cheap enough to buy, other fat substances are used in their preparation instead of that precious juice from olives. In southern Greece (and especially in the islands) pies are prepared almost exclusively with olive oil. However, the traditional pies of northern areas of Greece can very well be prepared with olive oil.

Pies are a staple among the immigrating population of northern Greece, the Sarakatsans, who used to cook them almost every day. They were the easiest solution for them as they could be prepared with the products they had ready at hand. Olive oil affects the quality of these dishes greatly and this is why the Sarakatsans themselves prefer to buy and use it in their pies. The pies suggested in this chapter are made with many different ingredients. Some of them, though, are very interesting, such as the olive oil pie (lathenia), which is traditional in the cuisine of some small islands in the Cyclades. The name alone shows the importance of olive oil in its preparation.

Cheese pie with olive oil

For the puff pastry:

1	egg
3	tbsps olive oil
½	teaspoon salt
1	cup flour
4-5	tbsps milk

For the filling:

½	kg feta cheese, crumbled
3	eggs
½	cup milk
4	tbsps olive oil
3-4	tbsps fine semolina

Prepare a dough with the ingredients for the pastry, cover and refrigerate for 30 minutes. (You can also use commercial pastry).
Prepare the filling: In a medium-size bowl combine feta cheese, beaten eggs, milk, olive oil and semolina. Blend

very well with a fork and refrigerate for 1 hour.

Remove dough from refrigerator and roll it out on a lightly floured surface to a circle, the size of a baking tray. Spread the puff pastry on the bottom of an oiled baking tray and place the filling on top. Baste gently with 1-2 beaten eggs and bake in moderate heat until golden brown, for about one hour. After it has cooled a little, cut into pieces and serve.

Olive oil pie (Lathenia) from the Cyclades

1,5	cup water
1,5	envelope active dry yeast
½	teaspoon salt
½	cup olive oil
800	grams flour (preferably wheat)
1	medium onion, grated
2-3	firm tomatoes, peeled, seeded and chopped
1	teaspoon dried oregano
100	grams feta cheese, crumbled (optional)

Dilute yeast in warm water, add half olive oil, salt and flour, a little at a time till you have a soft dough. Knead well.

Place the dough in the center of an oiled baking pan and spread all over the bottom of the pan with your oiled finger tips. Leave it in a warm place to rise until double in bulk and top with onion, tomato, oregano, (feta

cheese) and remaining olive oil. Bake in moderate heat for about 50 minutes.

Spinach-and-greens pie

For the filling:
    1   kg greens (spinach and other greens), finely chopped
    5-6 spring onions, finely chopped
    ½   cup dill, finely chopped
    ½   cup fennel, finely chopped
    ½   cup olive oil
          salt and pepper
    ½   cup ground toasted bread
    200 grams crumbled feta cheese

For the dough:
    ½   cup olive oil
    ½   cup water
          grated rind and juice of
          1 lemon, ½ teaspoon salt
    2   cups self-raising flour

Prepare hard paste with the above ingredients and refrigerate for 30 minutes. Wash and finely chop spinach and greens. Heat olive oil in a saucepan and soften greens on low heat for about 15 minutes. Drain completely and combine with a little salt, pepper, to desired taste, feta cheese and toasted bread crumbs. (You can omit feta cheese). Remove dough from refrigerator and divide into 2 balls, one a little bigger than the other one. Roll out the bigger part on a lightly floured surface into a circle, large enough to fit into the bottom of the pan and hang over its sides by about 2 cms. Place it carefully in oiled pan leaving 2 cm of dough hanging over the sides. Spread filling evenly on top. Roll out second dough ball into a circle the size of the pan and cover the filling. Bring dough hanging over the outer sides and inner sides of the pan together and pinch carefully to joint them. Baste with olive oil, mark pieces with a sharp knife and bake in moderate heat until golden brown, about one hour. Cool for at least 20 minutes before serving.

Courgette pie

For the filling:
1 kg courgettes
1   teaspoon salt
4 tbsps olive oil
1 medium onion, grated
1 green pepper, grated
½ cup finely chopped dill or mint
4 eggs
½ cup grated cheese
½ cup zwieback biscuit crumbs

For the phyllo paste:
½ cup olive oil
½ cup milk
½ teaspoon salt
½ kg self-raising flour

Grate courgettes the evening before, season with salt, put into a colander and allow them to drain very well. The following day, combine well with the rest of the ingredients and leave aside.

Prepare the dough for the phyllo: Beat olive oil, milk and salt and slowly add flour until you have soft dough. Divide into 2 balls, one a little bigger than the other one. This you roll out and place on the bottom of an oiled pan leaving 2 cm dough hanging over the sides, as in the above recipe. Spread courgette mixture on top and cover with another phyllo, which you make by rolling out the remaining dough. Bring the dough hanging over the outer sides and inner sides of the pan together and pinch carefully to joint them. Baste with beaten egg, mark pieces with a sharp knife and bake in moderate heat until golden brown, about one hour.

Cheese bread

3   tbsps olive oil
1   cup water
250 grams crumbled feta cheese
1   package dry yeast
½   kg flour

Dilute yeast in lukewarm water, add olive oil and flour little by little until
you have a soft dough which doesn't stick to the hands. Add feta cheese
and knead to combine it with the dough. Place in an oiled bread pan,
press with your finger tips and leave it rise until double in bulk.
In the meantime preheat oven to 180 C. Baste cheese bread with an egg
beaten with a little olive oil and bake in moderate heat for about half an
hour.

Baked cheese pasties

For the puff pastry:
½   cup yoghurt
½   teaspoon baking soda
½   cup olive oil
½   teaspoon salt
    juice of 1 orange
½   kg flour

For the filling:
350 grams crumbled
    feta cheese
1   egg

Prepare the dough: Beat olive
oil with yoghurt, add baking soda diluted
in orange juice, salt and flour little by little
until you achieve a soft and elastic dough.
Combine feta cheese and egg for the filling. Take
pieces of dough the size of a walnut and roll each one
out into a small circle. Place 1 teaspoon filling on one half and
cover with the other half. Press the edges down with a fork to close firmly,
baste with beaten egg white and bake in moderate heat until golden brown,
about 25 minutes.

Spinach-and-greens pasties

For the puff pastry:
½   cup water
5   tbsps olive oil
1-2 eggs
1   teaspoon salt
½   kg self-rising flour

For the filling:

1   kg spinach
1   medium onion or 5 spring
    onions, finely chopped
4   tbsps olive oil
1   cup finely chopped parsley
½   cup grated kefalotyri (*hard
    cheese made from sheep's milk*)
    or crumbled feta cheese
½   teaspoon salt, pepper

Beat eggs, add olive oil, water, salt
and finally flour, little by little. Knead
till you have a hard and elastic dough.
Cover and refrigerate for 30 minutes.
Prepare the filling: wash and chop spinach,
dip in boiling water for 5 minutes and then drain completely. Heat olive
oil in a saucepan and soften onion. Add spinach and stir a few times until
juice has evaporated. Put in parsley, salt and pepper, remove from heat
and stir in kefalotyri cheese or feta cheese.
Take pieces of dough the size of a walnut and roll each one out into a
small circle. Place 1 teaspoon filling on one half and cover with the other
half. Press the edges down with a fork to close firmly, baste with olive
oil or beaten egg white and bake in moderate heat until golden brown,
about 25 minutes.

Rice pie

½   kg rice
8   eggs
400 grams grated cheese
½   cup olive oil
½   kg commercial pastry

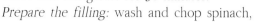

Put enough water in a large pot, bring
to a boil and cook rice for 5 minutes. Place rice in a colander, rinse with
cold water under the tap and allow it to drain well. Combine with beaten
eggs, salt, cheese and 3 tbsps olive oil.
Layer 3 pastry sheets in an oiled baking tray, one at a time, brushing each
one with olive oil. Spread about one third of the filling over the last sheet.
Repeat twice and finish by placing 4 pastry sheets on top, brushed again
with olive oil. Cut into serving portions with a sharp knife and bake in
preheated oven (180° C.) till golden brown, about 1 hour.

VEGETABLES AND OLIVE OIL

The Orthodox Church diet requires the consumption of great amounts of vegetables, as they are among the products which are allowed during the fasting periods. Thus, as time passed, a special dietary code was created which goes together with the rural as well as with the older customs. The consumption of vegetables almost always coincides with the consumption of olive oil. In Crete, which, as mentioned above, is considered to be a peak area for the Mediterranean diet, the consumption of vegetables is almost on an everyday basis. This, of course, doesn't suggest dietary monotony, but resourcefulness and inventiveness for unlimited food combinations. This happens because the Cretans do not consume only one (or just a few) kinds of vegetables. Their diet includes an incredible variety of vegetables which go very well with other food products.

Roasted potatoes with olive oil and oregano

1,5 kg potatoes
½ cup olive oil
1 teaspoon salt, pepper
2 teaspoons dried oregano
  juice of 2 lemons

Peel potatoes, cut lengthwise into 4 or more pieces and place in a baking tray. Sprinkle with salt, pepper, oregano, olive oil, lemon juice and 1 cup water. Bake in the oven, first in high temperature for 20 minutes and then in moderate heat for another 50 minutes until the potatoes are soft and golden brown.

Fried red peppers with yoghurt sauce

10 red peppers (peppers of Florina)
2 cloves of garlic
1 teaspoon salt
300 grams strained yoghurt
3 tbsps olive oil
1 tbsp. vinegar

Wash peppers, remove stems and seeds, pat dry with kitchen roll and fry or grill until their skin begins to blister.
Mash garlic with salt and mix with yoghurt. Add olive oil and vinegar and combine all ingredients together. Top red peppers with this sauce and serve.

Potato purée with olive oil

1 kg potatoes
3/4 cup olive oil (*preferably flavoured with thyme or other herbs*)
3/4 cup milk
1 teaspoon salt
freshly ground pepper
3/4 cup grated kefalotyri cheese
(*hard cheese made from sheep's milk*)

Boil potatoes, peel and mash in food processor.
Slowly add olive oil, milk, salt, pepper and cheese and continue puréeing until the mixture is smooth.

Baked aubergines with tomato sauce

2 large aubergines
3-4 medium-size potatoes
½ kg tomatoes, peeled, seeded and chopped
1 medium onion, finely chopped
3 tbsps olive oil
salt, pepper, cumin, oregano
150 grams crumbled feta cheese
1 cup olive oil for frying

Cut aubergines lengthwise into large oval slices and put in salted water for about one hour.
Slice the potatoes like the aubergines and fry until lightly brown. Drain on kitchen roll, place on oven tray in single layer and season with salt.
Drain aubergines completely, fry and drain again on kitchen roll. Place on top of potatoes and salt them, too.
To prepare the sauce: Heat 3 tbsps olive oil in a saucepan and soften the onion. Add tomatoes, very little salt, freshly ground pepper, cumin and oregano. Lower heat and simmer for about half an hour. When all liquid has been absorbed, remove pan from heat and stir in the feta cheese.
Top aubergines with sauce and bake in moderate heat for about half an hour.

Kritharokouloura (Rusks) with tomato and olive oil

About rusks, those coarse, toasted thick slices of bread, see more in the chapter about salads. The rusks used for this dish are usually round and made from barley or barley and wheat. Rusks seasoned with tomato and olive oil are very popular in Crete, but recently they've become popular in other parts of Greece, too.

2	thick barley or whole wheat paximathia (rusks)
2	ripe tomatoes, peeled, seeded and chopped
2	tbsps olive oil
	salt, oregano
100	grams crumbled feta cheese

Sprinkle rusks with very little water to dampen and soften slightly. Place each one on a plate, drizzle tomato, salt, olive oil, oregano and feta cheese and serve immediately. Alternatively you can break the rusk into chunks.

Spinach and yoghurt

300	grams spinach
1	onion, finely chopped
2	tbsps olive oil
2	tbsps coarsely ground walnuts or pine seeds (optional)
	salt and pepper, to taste
250	grams strained yoghurt
1	mashed garlic clove
1	tbsp. olive oil
1	tbsp. lemon juice

Wash and boil spinach for 3 minutes. Heat 2 tbsps olive oil in saucepan and brown onions until translucent. Drain spinach thoroughly and add to the pan. (If you use walnuts or pine-seeds, put them in the pan before the spinach). Season with salt and pepper and cook until almost all liquid has been absorbed. Serve spinach with yoghurt on top, which you combine well with garlic, salt, olive oil and lemon juice.

Aubergines stuffed with minced meat

6	large aubergines
6	tbsps olive oil
1	onion, coarsely chopped
250	grams minced meat (lamb and veal)
3	mashed garlic cloves
3-4	tbsps almonds, coarsely ground
4	medium tomatoes, peeled, seeded and chopped
	salt and pepper
½	teaspoon ground cinnamon
1	tbsp. parsley, finely chopped
1	tbsp. fresh mint, finely chopped
1	green pepper and 1 tomato

Wash aubergines, cut off their stems and make an incision lengthwise in each aubergine, being careful not to cut them through. Sprinkle with salt into the incisions and let them stand for 1-2 hours.
In a bowl combine well all the ingredients for the filling: minced meat, onion, garlic, almonds, tomatoes, 2 tbsps olive oil, salt, pepper, cinnamon, parsley and mint.
Drain aubergines and fry slightly on all sides. Place in a baking tray. Taking one aubergine at a time, carefully fill each slit with the minced meat mixture. Cut tomato and pepper into 6 slices each and put the slices on the aubergines. Pour over 4 tbsps olive oil and 4 tbsps water, cover the baking tray with aluminum foil and bake in moderate heat for half an hour. Remove the foil and bake for another 30 minutes.

Peppers stuffed with cheese

1	kg green long peppers
4	tbsps olive oil
½	cup crumbled feta cheese
½	cup grated kefalotyri (hard cheese made from sheep's milk)
1	onion, finely chopped
1	tbsp. parsley, finely chopped
1	teaspoon tomato paste diluted in ½ cup water
	pepper to taste

Wash peppers, remove stems and seeds and boil in water for 5 minutes. Drain completely and let them cool down. Heat olive oil in a saucepan, brown the onion and add tomato paste, parsley, feta cheese, kefalotyri cheese and pepper. Simmer for 5 minutes and remove from heat. Stuff peppers carefully with the mixture, put a chunk of bread in the opening and place them in a baking tray. Baste with a little olive oil and bake in preheated oven for about 40 minutes. Alternatively, you can fry them.

Stewed potatoes with onions

1,5	kg potatoes quartered
½	cup olive oil
3	medium onions, coarsely chopped
1	garlic clove, finely chopped
5	medium tomatoes peeled, seeded and chopped
2	bay leaves
	salt and pepper, to taste

Heat olive oil in a large pot and soften onions until they gain a little colour. Add garlic along with tomatoes, potatoes, bay leaves, salt, pepper and 2 cups water. Cover the pot and cook over medium to low heat for about 1 hour. Do not stir the food with a spoon, only shake the pot back and forth to prevent potatoes from getting burnt.
(This dish can also be cooked in the oven).

OLIVE OIL IN SWEETS

Even today, visitors to Crete are surprised when they realize that olive oil is used even in the preparation of sweets! Furthermore, in older times, when sugar was imported, therefore expensive, the only sweeteners used by Cretan housewives were grape-juice syrup and honey! Traditional sweets are prepared almost exclusively with olive oil.

Some people use refined olive oil to avoid the strong taste. We believe that, in sweets, too, an extra virgin olive oil is required, without a particularly characteristic taste or smell.

New Year's Cake with Olive oil

New Year's cake or Saint Basil's cake is the symbol of the Greek New Year's meal. It is either a cake, pie or bread prepared almost all over Greece, although in various ways. A coin is inserted before baking, and

whoever finds it in his/her slice is supposed to have good luck in the coming year. It is a survival of the sacred bread of Greek antiquity. Ancient Greeks used to offer such bread to the gods on great feast days. Later, during Roman Saturnalia (Greek celebrations in honour of Cronus), they cast lots to elect the "King of the celebration".

New Year's cake is cut by the head of the family and the first slice is for Christ, the second for the Virgin Mary, the third for Saint Basil, whose feast is on 1st January, and then there follow slices for the household and the members of the family.

- 1,5 cup olive oil
- 2 cups sugar
- 6 eggs
- ½ teaspoon vanilla extract or 50 ml brandy
  grated rind and juice of 2 medium oranges
- ½ cup milk
- ½ kg self-raising flour

Preheat oven to 180° C.

Beat olive oil with sugar and continue with yolks, vanilla or brandy, orange rind, orange juice, milk, flour and finally the egg whites beaten stiff. Combine carefully and pour the mixture into an oiled No 30 baking tin. Do not forget to insert a coin.

Bake in preheated oven (180° C) for about 1 hour without opening the oven door, at least during the first 40 minutes.

Baklavas with olive oil

A very popular Greek sweet which seems to have its roots in Ancient Greek gastronomy, when they used to wrap various ingredients in puff pastry and prepare sweets. Such a sweet was "Gastrin", which was mentioned by Athenaeus, a writer of Roman times, as a Cretan sweet.

1   kg roughly chopped walnuts
½   cup sugar
½   cup ground toasted bread
2   tbsps ground cinnamon and clove
½   kg commercial pastry
3/4 cup olive oil for basting the pastry sheets

Syrup:
1   cup honey
½   cup sugar
3/4 cup water
2   tbsps lemon juice

In a large bowl mix walnuts, toasted bread, sugar, cinnamon and clove powder.

Brush a rectangular oven tray with olive oil and place 4 pastry sheets, one at a time, brushing each one with olive oil. Spread about 1/3 of the nut mixture over the last sheet and place 2 pastry sheets over the nuts, one at a time, brushing again with olive oil. Continue in this manner till all the ingredients are used up. On top, place 4 pastry sheets, each one brushed with olive oil. Sprinkle the top sheet with a little water and olive oil.

Cut into serving portions with a sharp knife, first vertically and then horizontally. Bake in preheated oven (180° C.) till golden brown.

In the meantime prepare the syrup: In a large saucepan put sugar, honey, water and lemon juice and bring to a boil. Simmer for 10 minutes and pour hot syrup over hot baklavas, as soon as you remove it from oven.

Carrot cake with olive oil

½   cup olive oil
½   cup sugar
1   tbsp. ground cinnamon
1   teaspoon grated orange rind
3/4 cup fresh orange juice
½   cup grated carrot
½   cup grated apple
3/4 cup seedless raisins

½   cup coarsely ground walnuts
4   tbsps brandy
1,5 cup all purpose flour
2   teaspoons baking powder

Beat olive oil with sugar, add cinnamon powder, orange rind, orange juice, carrot, apple, raisins, baking powder diluted in brandy and finally flour. Combine well. Brush a baking pan with olive oil, pour mixture into it and bake in preheated oven (180º C.) for about 1 hour.

Yoghurt cake with olive oil

½   cup olive oil
1   cup sugar
5   eggs
250 grams yoghurt *(preferably strained yoghurt)*
3   teaspoons baking powder
1   teaspoon grated lemon rind
1,5 cup flour

Beat olive oil with sugar and continue by adding yolks, lemon rind, yoghurt, flour sifted with baking powder and finally egg whites beaten stiff. Combine very carefully and transfer the mixture into an oiled No 30 baking tin. Bake in preheated oven (180º C) for about one hour.

Raisin cake with olive oil

1,5 cup olive oil
1,5 cup sugar
2   cups fresh orange juice
2   teaspoons baking soda
1   cup liquid from boiled cinnamon or water
50   ml brandy
2   teasp. baking powder
1   tbsp ground cinnamon and clove
1   cup seedless raisins
1   teaspoon grated orange

rind
½   cup coarsely ground walnuts (optional)
1   kg all purpose flour

In a large bowl start beating olive oil and sugar and then add boiled cinnamon, baking soda diluted in orange juice, baking powder diluted in brandy, cinnamon and clove powder, orange rind, walnuts, raisins and finally flour, working the mixture as you go along.
Transfer the mixture into an oiled No 40 baking tin and bake in preheated oven (moderate heat) for 1 hour and 20 minutes.

Apple cake with olive oil

½   cup olive oil
1   cup sugar
5   eggs
1   tbsp ground cinnamon and clove powder
1   teaspoon baking soda
     juice of 1 lemon
3   tbsps brandy
1,5 cup all-purpose flour
2   teaspoons baking powder
1   kg apples, cut into thin slices
2   grated pears or 1 pear and 1 quince

Prepare the mixture: Beat olive oil with sugar, and continue with cinnamon and clove, egg yolks, baking soda diluted in lemon juice, baking powder diluted in brandy, flour and finally the egg whites beaten stiff. Combine carefully and pour half mixture in an oiled No 32 baking tin. Place fruit on top and pour the rest of the mixture on the fruit. Bake in moderate heat (preheated oven) for almost an hour.

Walnut cake with olive oil

- 1   cup olive oil
- 1   cup sugar
- 6   eggs
- 1   cup milk
- 1   tbsp ground cinnamon and clove
- 1   cup coarsely ground walnuts
- 3   cups all-purpose flour
- 3   teaspoons baking powder

Syrup:

- 1   cup sugar
- 1   tbsp honey
- ½   cup water
- 1   tbsp lemon juice

In a large bowl start beating olive oil with sugar and add yolks, cinnamon and clove, walnuts, baking powder diluted in milk and the flour, stirring the mixture continuously. In the end add egg whites which have been beaten very well and combine very carefully. Pour the mixture in an oiled No 32 baking tin and bake in moderate heat for about an hour. Remove the cake from oven and let it cool down a little.

Prepare the syrup: Put sugar, honey, water and lemon juice in a pot and boil for 10 minutes. Pour hot syrup over warm walnut cake.

(If desired, you can prepare a cream with milk and corn flour, spread it on top of the walnut cake and sprinkle with chopped walnuts).

Olive oil cake

1,5	cup olive oil
1,5	cup sugar
1	cup milk
4	eggs
2	teaspoons baking powder
	grated rind and juice of 1 lemon
1	teaspoon baking soda
1	tbsp ground cinnamon and clove
3,5	cups all-purpose flour

In a large bowl beat olive oil and sugar and continue by adding yolks, cinnamon and clove, lemon rind, baking soda diluted in lemon juice, baking powder diluted in milk, flour and finally egg whites beaten stiff. Combine the whites very carefully with the rest of the mixture, transfer in oiled No 32 baking pan and bake in preheated oven (moderate heat) for about an hour.

Chocolate cake

1	cup olive oil
1,5	cup sugar
5	eggs
1	cup milk
½	teaspoon vanilla extract
250	grams confectionery chocolate
½	kg self-raising flour

In a large bowl beat olive oil and sugar and continue by adding yolks, vanilla extract, milk, chocolate cut into small pieces, flour and finally egg whites beaten stiff. Pour mixture into oiled No 32 baking tin and bake in moderate heat (preheated oven) for a little less than an hour.

Kourambiethes (sugar-coated biscuits) with olive oil

Kourambiethes are the traditional Christmas sweets all over Greece. They are sold in Greek cake shops on those days or can be found packaged in supermarkets. In any case, it is customary to prepare kourambiethes at Christmas in every Greek house.

- 2 cups olive oil
- ½ cup sugar
- 4 tbsps brandy
- 1 tbsp ground cinnamon
- 1 whole egg and 1 yolk
- 1 cup almonds, roasted and coarsely ground
  all purpose flour (about 3 cups)
- 2-3 cups icing sugar

In a large bowl beat olive oil and sugar thoroughly and continue with eggs, brandy, cinnamon, almonds and slowly flour until you have soft dough which does not stick to the hands. Take pieces of dough the size of a walnut and shape round, oblong or oval kourambiethes. Place on oiled baking pan or on cookie sheet and bake in moderate heat for 15-20 minutes. Remove from oven, let kourambiethes cool slightly and sift icing sugar over them until they are completely covered.

Raisin biscuits

- 1 cup olive oil
- ½ cup sugar
- 1 teaspoon ground cinnamon
- ½ teaspoon ground clove
- 1 teaspoon grated orange rind
- 1 teaspoon baking soda
- ½ cup fresh orange juice
- 1 teaspoon baking powder
- 3 tbsps brandy
- ½ cup almonds or walnuts, coarsely ground
- 1 cup seedless raisins (sultanas)
- ½ kg all-purpose flour

Dust raisins with a little flour and mash in food processor for 5 minutes. In a large bowl beat olive oil and sugar and add cinnamon, clove, orange

rind, baking soda diluted in orange juice, baking powder diluted in brandy, almonds or walnuts, raisins and slowly the flour until the dough becomes soft and smooth. Take pieces of dough the size of a walnut and shape round biscuits. Place on baking sheet and bake in moderate heat for 20 minutes or until they are golden brown.

Honey biscuits (Melomakarona)

Melomakarona, like kourambiethes, are traditional Christmas sweets.

2	cups olive oil
½	cup caster sugar
2	tbsps honey
1	teaspoon baking soda
1	teaspoon baking powder
2	cups fresh orange and mandarin juice
1	teaspoon grated orange rind
1	tbsp cinnamon and clove powder
½	cup coarsely ground walnuts (optional)
1	cup fine semolina
1200 grams all-purpose flour	

Syrup:

1	cup honey
1	cup sugar
2	cups water
1	cup roasted and ground sesame seeds or walnuts
1	teaspoon ground cinnamon

In a large bowl beat olive oil with sugar and honey. Add orange rind, cinnamon and clove, baking soda and baking powder diluted in fruit juice, walnuts and semolina, beating all the while. Slowly add flour until the dough is soft and malleable. Cover and let the dough stand for 30 minutes before using. Take pieces of dough the size of a small egg and form rounded oblong melomakarona. Place on baking sheet and bake in moderate heat for about 20 minutes or until they are golden brown. Remove from oven and let them cool. While meloma-karona are cooling, prepare the syrup by combining sugar, honey and water in a pot and boiling them for 10 minutes. Reduce heat, dip melom-akarona in the syrup and allow them to soak up for 1 minute. Remove with a slotted spoon and place on a serving tray. Sprinkle when still wet with ground sesame seeds or walnuts and ground cinnamon.

Olive oil biscuits (Koulourakia)

3 cups olive oil
2 cups sugar
   juice of 1 medium orange and
   1 lemon
1 tbsp ground cinnamon
5 tbsps brandy
2 teaspoons baking powder
1 teaspoon baking soda
1 cup roasted sesame seeds
1200 grams all-purpose flour

In a large bowl beat olive oil and sugar until creamy. Add baking soda diluted in juice, cinnamon, baking powder diluted in brandy and sesame seeds, beating all the while. Slowly sift flour as much as needed until the dough is soft and elastic. Cover and put dough in refrigerator for 30 minutes. Take pieces of dough the size of a small walnut and roll into a rope. Join the ends to form circles and place koulourakia on baking sheet. Bake in moderate heat for 20 minutes, until golden brown.

Semolina pudding (Chalvas)

1   cup olive oil
2   cups fine semolina
2,5 cups sugar
4   cups water
½   cup seedless raisins (optional)
1   bsp ground cinnamon
½   cup roasted chopped walnuts

In a pot, over medium heat, bring sugar and water to a boil and simmer for 10 minutes. Remove from heat, add raisins and let syrup cool slightly. In a large pot heat olive oil until it begins to sizzle. Slowly add semolina, stirring constantly for about 10 minutes with a wooden spoon until semolina is lightly brown. Add walnuts and then the syrup very slowly stirring constantly and being careful not to burn yourself as the mixture will bubble. Stir over low heat for about 10 minutes, until the syrup is completely absorbed by the semolina. Remove from heat and pour chalvas in a large mold or in several small ones. Sprinkle with ground cinnamon and walnuts, if desired.
(Instead of raisins you can add dried plums or crystallized fruit. You can substitute walnuts with almonds or pine seeds).

Raisin Bread

4   envelopes of dry active yeast
½   cup olive oil
1   cup sugar
½   cup fresh orange juice
1   cup seedless raisins
1   teaspoon ground cinnamon
½   teaspoon ground mastic
2   kg all-purpose flour

In a medium bowl dilute the yeast in 1 cup lukewarm water.
Dust raisins with a little flour and put aside.
In a large bowl sift together flour and sugar, make a well in the centre and add diluted yeast, olive oil, orange juice, cinnamon, mastic and raisins. Stirring constantly, add lukewarm water (about 2 cups) until soft and elastic dough is formed. Cover and let it rise until double in size, about 1-2 hours. Divide into balls, the size you want and shape oblong loaves. Place in bread tins, cover with towel and allow them to rise again until double in size. Brush with milk or beaten egg and bake in moderate heat for 40-45 minutes, until golden brown.

Orange biscuits

2   cups olive oil
2   cups sugar
1   cup fresh orange juice
1   tbsp ground cinnamon and clove
1   tbsp baking powder
1   teaspoon baking soda
1   kg all-purpose flour (more or less)

In a large bowl beat olive oil and sugar until creamy. Add cinnamon and clove, baking soda diluted in orange juice and finally flour sifted together with baking powder stirring constantly until a dough begins to form. Knead well until the dough is soft and elastic and doesn't stick to the hands. Cover with a towel, refrigerate for half an hour and then shape the biscuits: Take pieces of dough the size of a walnut and roll into a rope. Join the ends to form circles and place koulourakia on cookie sheet. Bake in moderate heat for 20 minutes until golden brown.

Unsweetened biscuits

1   cup olive oil
1   teaspoon salt
1,5   cup grated cheese
½   kg self-raising flour

Combine the above ingredients in a large bowl and knead to a soft and elastic dough.
Shape the biscuits as above, brush with beaten egg, sprinkle with sesame seeds and bake in moderate heat for 15-20 minutes, until golden brown.

Dry measures
1 cup flour = 150 grams
1 cup semolina or caster sugar = 130 grams
1 cup sugar = 230 grams
1 cup rice = 230 grams
1 cup grated cheese = 100 grams
1 cup chopped almonds or walnuts = 100 grams

Liquids
1 cup = 225 ml
1 cup = 16 tablespoons (tbsps)
1 tablespoon = 3 teaspoons
1 tablespoon = 15 ml
1 teaspoon = 5 ml